THIS **journal** BELONGS TO

_____

_____

_____

MY GARDEN

MY GARDEN

A Five-Year Journal

MIMI LUEBBERMANN

CHRONICLE BOOKS

SAN FRANCISCO

MY THANKS GO TO BILL LEBLOND,
WHO WAS KIND ENOUGH TO THINK OF ME FOR THIS PROJECT.

A book, like a garden, benefits from the comfort of many caring hands.
Kate Woodrow, my editor, has been generous with her ideas, like seeds,
while Laura Harger, the copy editor, and Amy Bauman, the
proofreader, pruned and snipped to bring accuracy and clarity to the
text. Ann Spradlin and Doug Ogan shepherded the project through
its many stages with surefooted swiftness. Designer Andrew Schapiro
laid out the design like the bones of the garden, marrying together the
text with the evocative photos of Susie Cushner.

WITH THIS JOURNAL, WE SEND OUR HOPE TO GARDENERS EVERYWHERE THAT
WORKING THE SOIL TO MAKE GARDENS WILL GIVE SOLACE AND BALANCE TO AN
EVER-INCREASING TECHNOLOGICAL LIFE.

LIBRARY OF CONGRESS CATALOGING-IN-PUBLICATION DATA AVAILABLE.
ISBN: 978-0-8118-7446-5

MANUFACTURED IN CHINA
DESIGNED BY ANDREW SCHAPIRO
TEXT BY MIMI LUEBBERMANN

10 9 8 7 6 5 4 3

CHRONICLE BOOKS LLC
680 SECOND STREET
SAN FRANCISCO, CALIFORNIA 94107
WWW.CHRONICLEBOOKS.COM

CONTENTS

How to Use This
JOURNAL

Gardeners are optimists, saying, despite failed harvests, insect plagues, erratic weather, and everything else that can (and will) go awry, "Well, there's always next year." Unstated in that brief sentence is our fervent hope that perhaps next year the rain will fall gently on emerging daffodils, that early mulching will inhibit the riptide of incoming weeds, and that high winds will not blow over beanpoles.

Gardening is about being flexible. We also must juggle garden chores while maintaining our daily lives, and despite all best intentions, too often the urgent needs of the garden slip in priority below the demands of work, parenting, and other duties.

A garden journal can help immensely. This journal has been designed to assist you in many ways. Refer to its seasonal checklists and topical notes to prioritize the major tasks of each season and to anticipate future garden needs. Use the daily journal pages to jot down successes and failures, and even record the arrival of both pests and butterfly friends in the garden. Store photos of your garden or magazine clippings in the pocket at the back of the book. And play with the Garden Sketches pages to hone your vision of both your garden's current lines and plans for its future.

This planner is designed to help you enjoy five (or even more) years of progress in your garden. You can start recording at any time of year and continue through the seasons. To begin, take a few minutes drawing your garden on the sketching pages. This will help you remember where your garden beds and plants are located when obscured by snow, which they usually will be just when you want to order seeds or buy bare-root plants to set in when the weather warms.

Check with a U.S. Department of Agriculture zone map online or in a garden book. It defines gardening areas according to their approximate average range of temperatures. Locate your garden area on the map but realize that each garden has its own microclimate, so average temperatures may vary in your garden. Record your garden's daily highs and lows in this journal to help fine-tune your knowledge of your USDA zone. The most important dates to record are those of the first and last frosts, as these will have a great impact on the garden.

Each seasonal section includes brief topical notes intended to inspire and instruct you through the season, plus tips and hints that will enrich your knowledge. If you're looking for more guidance, many of these topics, such as those on soil, fertilizers, growing and drying herbs, and more, are expanded on in the Planting Primer appendix.

Keep your journal in a handy place—on your nightstand or a kitchen shelf—where it's easy to find, so you'll remember to jot down new plantings, temperatures, and garden discoveries. Make an effort to write notes or sketch as regularly as possible. In the years to come, your past references will provide a guide to new ideas, different plantings, and, above all, they will remind you of the joy your garden brings, from the discovery of the first blooming daffodil in the spring to the last pink colchicum popping out of the ground in the fall.

SPRING

*Poets may describe spring as gently
veiling the hills in emerald green,
but for the gardener, spring vibrates
with the tension of a coiled spring.*

SUDDENLY there is an urgent amount of work to do in the garden, and every inch of ground seems to beg for attention. Baby seed starts yearn to be placed in their garden beds, bare-root fruit trees should be planted out in the orchard, pruning must be finished and the trimmings ground up for compost, and weeding has to begin.

In early spring, map out your garden plans and strategize on when to dig, weed, plant, and prune. Six to eight weeks before you expect your last frost, plant seeds indoors in containers, using horticultural heat mats if possible to make sure they get plenty of bottom heat and placing the pots where they will get generous amounts of light.

Gardeners in cold-winter areas need to prepare for spring by uncovering winter-protected shrubs, clearing away winter debris such as downed branches, and watching for emerging spikes of spring-blooming bulbs. In warmer garden climates, be cautious, as warm days may lure you into injudiciously planting tender seedlings that could be killed by late frosts. Use cold frames and hot boxes to protect plants in the chilly daytime air, or try row crop covers—specially woven material that holds in heat—in the vegetable garden to keep off the spring chill. Accustom greenhouse or indoor seedlings to the outdoors by hardening them off in cold frames or a protected outdoors spot before planting them out in the garden.

A week or so outside in light shade during the day should help them adjust, but remember to bring them inside at night. Last, test the soil. If the soil falls off the back of a shovel in a clump, it is too wet to work without harming its composition.

In all the hectic swirl of spring, don't forget that as the garden wakes up from winter, you must carefully pace yourself as your body regains its fitness for bending to pull weeds, stretching to saw branches, and laboring to shovel in new bare-root plants.

SPRING

TEMPERATURE A.M.:

TEMPERATURE P.M.:

WEATHER BRIEFS:

GARDEN VISITORS *(birds, insects, critters)*:

COLOR IN THE GARDEN:

SPECIAL PLEASURES:

LESSONS LEARNED:

TRIUMPHS:

DON'T FORGET:

PLAN AHEAD:

NOTES:

SPRING

DATE:

TEMPERATURE A.M.:

TEMPERATURE P.M.:

WEATHER BRIEFS:

GARDEN VISITORS *(birds, insects, critters)*:

COLOR IN THE GARDEN:

SPECIAL PLEASURES:

LESSONS LEARNED:

TRIUMPHS:

DON'T FORGET:

PLAN AHEAD:

NOTES:

SPRING

DATE:

TEMPERATURE A.M.:

TEMPERATURE P.M.:

WEATHER BRIEFS:

GARDEN VISITORS *(birds, insects, critters)*:

COLOR IN THE GARDEN:

SPECIAL PLEASURES:

LESSONS LEARNED:

TRIUMPHS:

DON'T FORGET:

PLAN AHEAD:

NOTES:

SPRING

DATE: _____

TEMPERATURE A.M.: _____

TEMPERATURE P.M.: _____

WEATHER BRIEFS: _____

GARDEN VISITORS *(birds, insects, critters)*: _____

_____

_____

_____

_____

COLOR IN THE GARDEN: _____

_____

_____

_____

_____

SPECIAL PLEASURES: _____

_____

LESSONS LEARNED: _____

_____

TRIUMPHS: _____

_____

DON'T FORGET: _____

_____

PLAN AHEAD: _____

_____

NOTES: _____

_____

_____

_____

_____

_____

_____

SPRING

TEMPERATURE A.M.:

TEMPERATURE P.M.:

WEATHER BRIEFS:

GARDEN VISITORS *(birds, insects, critters)*:

COLOR IN THE GARDEN:

SPECIAL PLEASURES:

LESSONS LEARNED:

TRIUMPHS:

DON'T FORGET:

PLAN AHEAD:

NOTES:

SPRING

DATE:

TEMPERATURE A.M.:   TEMPERATURE P.M.:

WEATHER BRIEFS: GARDEN VISITORS *(birds, insects, critters)*:

COLOR IN THE GARDEN:

SPECIAL PLEASURES:

LESSONS LEARNED:

TRIUMPHS:

DON'T FORGET:

PLAN AHEAD:

NOTES:

SPRING

DATE:

TEMPERATURE A.M.:

TEMPERATURE P.M.:

WEATHER BRIEFS:

GARDEN VISITORS *(birds, insects, critters)*:

COLOR IN THE GARDEN:

SPECIAL PLEASURES:

LESSONS LEARNED:

TRIUMPHS:

DON'T FORGET:

PLAN AHEAD:

NOTES:

SPRING

DATE: _____

TEMPERATURE A.M.: _____

WEATHER BRIEFS: _____
_____
_____

COLOR IN THE GARDEN: _____
_____
_____

SPECIAL PLEASURES: _____
_____

LESSONS LEARNED: _____
_____

TRIUMPHS: _____
_____

DON'T FORGET: _____
_____

PLAN AHEAD: _____
_____

NOTES: _____
_____
_____
_____
_____
_____

TEMPERATURE P.M.: _____

GARDEN VISITORS *(birds, insects, critters)*: _____
_____
_____
_____
_____
_____

SPRING

DATE:

TEMPERATURE A.M.:

TEMPERATURE P.M.:

WEATHER BRIEFS:

GARDEN VISITORS *(birds, insects, critters)*:

COLOR IN THE GARDEN:

SPECIAL PLEASURES:

LESSONS LEARNED:

TRIUMPHS:

DON'T FORGET:

PLAN AHEAD:

NOTES:

DATE: _____

TEMPERATURE A.M.: _____

TEMPERATURE P.M.: _____

WEATHER BRIEFS: _____

GARDEN VISITORS *(birds, insects, critters)*:

COLOR IN THE GARDEN: _____

SPECIAL PLEASURES: _____

LESSONS LEARNED: _____

TRIUMPHS: _____

DON'T FORGET: _____

PLAN AHEAD: _____

NOTES: _____

PLANT BULBS NOW
FOR SUMMER COLOR

Summer-blooming bulbs can rescue a garden depleted of its spring bloom and slipping into monochrome green. Bulb companies ship roots and bulbs in early March or at a time suitable to your growing climate. Gladiolas, crocosmia, calla lilies, canna lilies, and dahlias are a few summer bulbs with a great variety of form and color. Consider the species gladiola, hard to find in catalogs but easy to naturalize in the garden, particularly in the western states. Look for fall-blooming crocus for spectacular blooms at the end of the garden season. Some bulbs require summer water, while others are drought tolerant, but they all provide reliable color in the summer garden.

The glory of spring-blooming bulbs, while brilliant, fades quickly. All too soon you will be left with untidy foliage topped by brown, spent blooms. The impulse is to deadhead (a gardener's grim term for trimming off the blossoms) and snip off the foliage at the same time, but don't! This will kill the bulbs. The leaves manufacture the nutrition required to produce blooms the following year. Cut bulb leaves off only when they have yellowed and withered.

SPRING

DATE:

TEMPERATURE A.M.:

TEMPERATURE P.M.:

WEATHER BRIEFS:

GARDEN VISITORS *(birds, insects, critters)*:

COLOR IN THE GARDEN:

SPECIAL PLEASURES:

LESSONS LEARNED:

TRIUMPHS:

DON'T FORGET:

PLAN AHEAD:

NOTES:

SPRING

DATE:

TEMPERATURE A.M.:

TEMPERATURE P.M.:

WEATHER BRIEFS:

GARDEN VISITORS *(birds, insects, critters)*:

COLOR IN THE GARDEN:

SPECIAL PLEASURES:

LESSONS LEARNED:

TRIUMPHS:

DON'T FORGET:

PLAN AHEAD:

NOTES:

SPRING

DATE:

TEMPERATURE A.M.:

TEMPERATURE P.M.:

WEATHER BRIEFS:

GARDEN VISITORS *(birds, insects, critters)*:

COLOR IN THE GARDEN:

SPECIAL PLEASURES:

LESSONS LEARNED:

TRIUMPHS:

DON'T FORGET:

PLAN AHEAD:

NOTES:

SPRING

DATE:

TEMPERATURE A.M.: _____

TEMPERATURE P.M.: _____

WEATHER BRIEFS: _____

GARDEN VISITORS *(birds, insects, critters)*: _____

_____

_____

_____

_____

COLOR IN THE GARDEN: _____

_____

_____

_____

_____

SPECIAL PLEASURES: _____

_____

LESSONS LEARNED: _____

_____

TRIUMPHS: _____

_____

DON'T FORGET: _____

_____

PLAN AHEAD: _____

_____

NOTES: _____

_____

_____

_____

_____

_____

SPRING

DATE:

TEMPERATURE A.M.:

WEATHER BRIEFS:

COLOR IN THE GARDEN:

SPECIAL PLEASURES:

LESSONS LEARNED:

TRIUMPHS:

DON'T FORGET:

PLAN AHEAD:

NOTES:

TEMPERATURE P.M.:

GARDEN VISITORS *(birds, insects, critters)*:

SPRING

DATE: _____

TEMPERATURE A.M.: _____

WEATHER BRIEFS: _____

_____

_____

COLOR IN THE GARDEN: _____

_____

_____

SPECIAL PLEASURES: _____

_____

LESSONS LEARNED: _____

_____

TRIUMPHS: _____

_____

DON'T FORGET: _____

_____

PLAN AHEAD: _____

_____

NOTES: _____

_____

_____

_____

_____

_____

_____

TEMPERATURE P.M.: _____

GARDEN VISITORS *(birds, insects, critters)*: _____

_____

_____

_____

_____

_____

_____

GROW YOUR GARDEN
WITH CONTAINERS

Not many gardeners have more than a tidy back pocket of space for a garden paradise, but containers can stretch your garden ground, highlight a rare or unusual plant, and provide a visual highlight in a border. Plants in containers depend upon you for food and water, so they require more care: monthly feedings and, in hot weather, almost daily watering. Cast-off olive oil cans, rickety wheelbarrows, even old shoes filled with potting soil all add a whimsical note to container collections. Once spring bulbs grown in containers have bloomed out, they are easy to whisk away to an out-of-sight location to finish up their cycle. Make sure your containers have holes drilled in the bottom for drainage, or, insert a pot with a drainage hole into the display pot—one without a hole—adding rocks to the bottom of the display pot. This lifts the plant's container above any water left from watering, so that your plant doesn't stay soggy from lack of drainage, a sure way to kill off the roots.

SPRING

TEMPERATURE A.M.: _____

TEMPERATURE P.M.: _____

WEATHER BRIEFS: _____

GARDEN VISITORS *(birds, insects, critters)*: _____

_____

_____

COLOR IN THE GARDEN: _____

_____

_____

SPECIAL PLEASURES: _____

LESSONS LEARNED: _____

TRIUMPHS: _____

DON'T FORGET: _____

PLAN AHEAD: _____

NOTES: _____

_____

_____

_____

_____

_____

SPRING

DATE:

TEMPERATURE A.M.:

TEMPERATURE P.M.:

WEATHER BRIEFS:

GARDEN VISITORS *(birds, insects, critters)*:

COLOR IN THE GARDEN:

SPECIAL PLEASURES:

LESSONS LEARNED:

TRIUMPHS:

DON'T FORGET:

PLAN AHEAD:

NOTES:

SPRING

DATE:

TEMPERATURE A.M.:

TEMPERATURE P.M.:

WEATHER BRIEFS:

GARDEN VISITORS *(birds, insects, critters)*:

COLOR IN THE GARDEN:

SPECIAL PLEASURES:

LESSONS LEARNED:

TRIUMPHS:

DON'T FORGET:

PLAN AHEAD:

NOTES:

SPRING

DATE:

TEMPERATURE A.M.:

TEMPERATURE P.M.:

WEATHER BRIEFS:

GARDEN VISITORS *(birds, insects, critters)*:

COLOR IN THE GARDEN:

SPECIAL PLEASURES:

LESSONS LEARNED:

TRIUMPHS:

DON'T FORGET:

PLAN AHEAD:

NOTES:

SPRING

DATE: _____

TEMPERATURE A.M.: _____

TEMPERATURE P.M.: _____

WEATHER BRIEFS: _____

GARDEN VISITORS *(birds, insects, critters)*: _____

_____

_____

COLOR IN THE GARDEN: _____

_____

_____

_____

SPECIAL PLEASURES: _____

_____

LESSONS LEARNED: _____

_____

TRIUMPHS: _____

_____

DON'T FORGET: _____

_____

PLAN AHEAD: _____

_____

NOTES: _____

_____

_____

_____

_____

_____

SPRING

DATE: _____

TEMPERATURE A.M.: _____

TEMPERATURE P.M.: _____

WEATHER BRIEFS: _____

GARDEN VISITORS *(birds, insects, critters)*: _____

_____

_____

_____

COLOR IN THE GARDEN: _____

_____

_____

_____

_____

SPECIAL PLEASURES: _____

_____

LESSONS LEARNED: _____

_____

TRIUMPHS: _____

_____

DON'T FORGET: _____

_____

PLAN AHEAD: _____

_____

NOTES: _____

_____

_____

_____

_____

_____

SPRING

DATE:

TEMPERATURE A.M.:

WEATHER BRIEFS:

COLOR IN THE GARDEN:

SPECIAL PLEASURES:

LESSONS LEARNED:

TRIUMPHS:

DON'T FORGET:

PLAN AHEAD:

NOTES:

TEMPERATURE P.M.:

GARDEN VISITORS *(birds, insects, critters)*:

SPRING

DATE:

TEMPERATURE A.M.:

TEMPERATURE P.M.:

WEATHER BRIEFS:

GARDEN VISITORS *(birds, insects, critters)*:

COLOR IN THE GARDEN:

SPECIAL PLEASURES:

LESSONS LEARNED:

TRIUMPHS:

DON'T FORGET:

PLAN AHEAD:

NOTES:

SPRING

DATE: _____

TEMPERATURE A.M.: _____

WEATHER BRIEFS: _____

_____

_____

COLOR IN THE GARDEN: _____

_____

_____

SPECIAL PLEASURES: _____

_____

LESSONS LEARNED: _____

_____

TRIUMPHS: _____

_____

DON'T FORGET: _____

_____

PLAN AHEAD: _____

_____

NOTES: _____

_____

_____

_____

_____

_____

TEMPERATURE P.M.: _____

GARDEN VISITORS *(birds, insects, critters)*:

_____

_____

_____

_____

_____

_____

_____

TEMPERATURE A.M.:

TEMPERATURE P.M.:

WEATHER BRIEFS:

GARDEN VISITORS *(birds, insects, critters)*:

COLOR IN THE GARDEN:

SPECIAL PLEASURES:

LESSONS LEARNED:

TRIUMPHS:

DON'T FORGET:

PLAN AHEAD:

NOTES:

SAVE MONEY WITH
BARE-ROOT PLANTS

Nurseries and catalogs offer bare-root plants from mid-winter to early spring. Because they come with no soil covering—often just sawdust and a plastic sleeve—bare-root plants will save you a lot of money. Shop early for the best selection. Look for deciduous fruit, nut, and shade trees; deciduous shrubs; roses; and berries offered as bare root. These plants are dormant (not actively growing) in winter, so they don't—at this point—need nourishment.

Because you take the plants home with their roots just barely covered with sand or sawdust, you must make sure that their roots do not dry out. Plant them within a day or so. Should that prove impossible due to schedule, weather, or soil conditions, then you can temporarily pot the plants in a container or cover the roots with a mound of damp soil. If the roots dry out, the plants will die.

SPRING

DATE:

TEMPERATURE A.M.: _____

TEMPERATURE P.M.: _____

WEATHER BRIEFS: _____

GARDEN VISITORS *(birds, insects, critters)*: _____

COLOR IN THE GARDEN: _____

SPECIAL PLEASURES: _____

LESSONS LEARNED: _____

TRIUMPHS: _____

DON'T FORGET: _____

PLAN AHEAD: _____

NOTES: _____

SPRING

DATE: _____

TEMPERATURE A.M.: _____   TEMPERATURE P.M.: _____

WEATHER BRIEFS: _____   GARDEN VISITORS *(birds, insects, critters)*: _____

_____   _____

_____   _____

COLOR IN THE GARDEN: _____   _____

_____   _____

_____   _____

SPECIAL PLEASURES: _____

_____

LESSONS LEARNED: _____

_____

TRIUMPHS: _____

_____

DON'T FORGET: _____

_____

PLAN AHEAD: _____

_____

NOTES: _____

_____

_____

_____

_____

_____

SPRING

DATE:

TEMPERATURE A.M.:

TEMPERATURE P.M.:

WEATHER BRIEFS:

GARDEN VISITORS *(birds, insects, critters)*:

COLOR IN THE GARDEN:

SPECIAL PLEASURES:

LESSONS LEARNED:

TRIUMPHS:

DON'T FORGET:

PLAN AHEAD:

NOTES:

SPRING

DATE: _____

TEMPERATURE A.M.: _____   TEMPERATURE P.M.: _____

WEATHER BRIEFS: _____   GARDEN VISITORS *(birds, insects, critters)*:

_____   _____

_____   _____

COLOR IN THE GARDEN: _____   _____

_____   _____

_____   _____

SPECIAL PLEASURES: _____

_____

LESSONS LEARNED: _____

_____

TRIUMPHS: _____

_____

DON'T FORGET: _____

_____

PLAN AHEAD: _____

_____

NOTES: _____

_____

_____

_____

_____

_____

_____

LET THE
GOOD BUGS BITE

Many a bug shares the gardener's harvest, much to the detriment of beloved plants. Earwigs nibble down a perfect rose blossom, Japanese beetles do their best to eat everything, and squash vine borers love to tunnel through stems, causing the vine to collapse. These pests need to be taken care of, and inviting good bugs into your garden can help. Spotted ladybug beetles are the rock stars of the helpful bugs, feeding on aphids and mites, but there are also the voracious lacewings, whose larvae feed on just about every plant-damaging insect. The larvae hatch into lacy-winged flying bugs attracted to nectar plants. Also for sale are the praying mantis egg cases, which hatch out hundreds of ravenous bug-eating machines. To maintain a healthy population of helpful bugs, do not use any pesticides or herbicides.

TAKE A TOUR

Every gardener needs inspiration, and in the spring, garden clubs, public gardens, and historic properties tidy up after winter and celebrate the new growing year. Use these tours and exhibitions to note plants that are successful under your local conditions, and to glean useful ideas on plant combinations.

DATE:

TEMPERATURE A.M.:

TEMPERATURE P.M.:

WEATHER BRIEFS:

GARDEN VISITORS *(birds, insects, critters)*:

COLOR IN THE GARDEN:

SPECIAL PLEASURES:

LESSONS LEARNED:

TRIUMPHS:

DON'T FORGET:

PLAN AHEAD:

NOTES:

SPRING

DATE:

TEMPERATURE A.M.:

TEMPERATURE P.M.:

WEATHER BRIEFS:

GARDEN VISITORS *(birds, insects, critters)*:

COLOR IN THE GARDEN:

SPECIAL PLEASURES:

LESSONS LEARNED:

TRIUMPHS:

DON'T FORGET:

PLAN AHEAD:

NOTES:

SPRING

DATE:

TEMPERATURE A.M.: _____

TEMPERATURE P.M.: _____

WEATHER BRIEFS: _____

GARDEN VISITORS *(birds, insects, critters)*: _____

COLOR IN THE GARDEN: _____

SPECIAL PLEASURES: _____

LESSONS LEARNED: _____

TRIUMPHS: _____

DON'T FORGET: _____

PLAN AHEAD: _____

NOTES: _____

SPRING

DATE: _____

TEMPERATURE A.M.: _____

WEATHER BRIEFS: _____

_____

_____

COLOR IN THE GARDEN: _____

_____

_____

SPECIAL PLEASURES: _____

_____

LESSONS LEARNED: _____

_____

TRIUMPHS: _____

_____

DON'T FORGET: _____

_____

PLAN AHEAD: _____

_____

NOTES: _____

_____

_____

_____

_____

_____

TEMPERATURE P.M.: _____

GARDEN VISITORS *(birds, insects, critters)*: _____

_____

_____

_____

_____

_____

Gardener's Spring
CHECKLIST

- ○ Prune and shape early-blooming shrubs after bloom.

- ○ Fertilize trees and shrubs when new growth starts.

- ○ Deadhead spring-blooming bulbs but do not cut off foliage until it has yellowed and withered.

- ○ Plant cool-weather crops such as radishes, peas, spinach, and lettuce.

- ○ Start seeds of summer-blooming annuals indoors six weeks before the date of the last frost, noted in your journal the preceding year.

- ○ Plant summer-blooming bulbs such as agapanthus, crinum, dahlia, canna, begonia, and gladiolus.

- ○ Tune up the lawn mower by the first day of spring.

- ○ On mother's day, plant warm-weather vegetables such as corn, beans, cucumbers, melons, okra, and squash in garden beds.

- ○ Check irrigation lines and drip hoses to prepare for early hot spells.

- ○ Foliar spray, that is, spray diluted fertilizer, on the foliage of garlic plants in march and april and maintain watering for the maximum bulb size. Stop watering when foliage tips begin to turn brown to allow bulbs to harden and mature.

- ○ Check with your nursery or plant stores to purchase pheromone traps for apple trees. These traps have a sticky interior to catch pesty coddling moths that will lay eggs in growing apples and hatch out into worms that ruin your apple crop. Attach them to limbs of the apple trees when the blossoms are just emerging.

○ Tune up the lawn mower by the first day of spring.

○ Prune and shape early-blooming shrubs after bloom.

○ Fertilize trees and shrubs when new growth starts.

○ Attach pheromone traps to apple trees just at blossom break.

○ Deadhead spring-blooming bulbs but do not cut off foliage until it has yellowed and withered.

○ Start seeds of summer-blooming annuals indoors six weeks before the date of the last frost, noted in your journal the preceding year.

○ Finish planting summer annuals and vegetables by June 1.

○ Start heat-loving annuals in garden beds.

○ Fill containers with tuberous begonias and plant lilies for a summer display.

○ During hot spells, make sure to water roses.

○ Plant autumn-blooming crocus for a fall display of white or pink flowers.

○ Plant summer vegetables after the last frost date for your microclimate. Stake tomatoes when planting.

○ Stay ahead of the weeds and mulch garden beds to inhibit further growth. Where possible, layer newspaper or weed cloth under mulch to deter the most persistent weeds.

○ Foliar spray (that is, spray diluted fertilizer) garlic in march and april and maintain watering for the maximum bulb size. Stop watering when tips begin to turn brown to allow bulbs to harden and mature.

○ Check trees and shrubs for winter storm damage and prune any broken limbs.

○ Prepare summer flower and vegetable beds by weeding and adding fertilizer and compost.

○ Transplant annual flower starts and summer vegetable seedlings to garden beds after the threat of frost has passed.

○ Divide winter-blooming perennials after bloom finishes. Using a sharp knife or shovel, cut through the center of the plant, making sure each half has plenty of roots. Gently lift one half of the plant and set in another spot. Fill the hole with soil and gently tamp down remaining half of plant.

○ Plant out summer bulbs, such as caladium, canna, and begonia, after the last frost.

○ Finish deadheading spring-blooming bulbs but do not cut off foliage until it has yellowed and withered.

○ Do not forget to prune fuchsias before their growth begins.

○ Fertilize citrus plants and palm trees.

○ Make sure to clean up dropped blossoms under camellias, as the decomposing blooms can spread camellia petal blight. Fertilize with an acid plant food after bloom has finished.

○ Divide crowded perennials.

○ Remove winter mulches from roses and other tender plants.

○ Sow seeds indoors for tomatoes, peppers, eggplants, melons, squash, and other warm-weather vegetables six weeks before the last frost date in your microclimate.

○ Harvest asparagus spears, cutting the stalk off under ground level but being careful not to injure the crown. Continue harvesting until the spears thin to less than ½ inch.

○ Prune and shape early-blooming shrubs after bloom.

○ Fertilize trees and shrubs when new growth starts.

○ Cut back ornamental grasses to 6 inches before new growth starts.

○ Sow sweet peas along the edge of a porch or a walkway. Provide support for sprawling plants. Use large tomato hoops, create a bamboo trellis, or string netting for the twining tendrils to catch hold of and climb up to bring their sweetly scented blossoms to eye-level.

○ Plant containers of red and white begonias with blue lobelia to celebrate when the Fourth of July rolls around.

○ Attach pheromone traps to apple trees just at the blossom break.

GARDEN SKETCHES

GARDEN SKETCHES

GARDEN SKETCHES

SUMMER

*Summer is excess
that erases the memory
of winter's icy penury.*

SUMMER in the garden is a time of extravagant abundance: baskets filled with sun-ripened fruit, waves of flowery perfume in warm air, sprawling melon vines, and long days that fade into starry nights.

Gardeners need to be advised to slow down in summer. Bask in summer's heat like a turtle on a log, but when working in the garden, start early and quit before the peak heat of the day or begin late in the afternoon, when the evening breeze brings down the temperature. Be sensible: wear a hat, drink lots of water when working outside, and use sunscreen to protect yourself from the sun's blistering rays.

Try to come up with strategies that will prevent you from resenting the demands of the summer garden so you can take the time to enjoy the garden in its fullness of bloom. Mulching in early summer slows weeds, which are as eager to grow as desirable plants. A timed watering system—whether a water-efficient drip structure, an overhead sprinkler head, or a combination of the two—will free you from the task of keeping the garden watered during hot, dry periods. Plant a vegetable garden but confine it to a sensible size for your household needs. For even though it may seem, in early spring, that five zucchini plants will be barely sufficient, an overabundance of produce will create extra work. Plant an extra row to supply your local food bank with produce but make a note of all your plantings, both the varieties and the quantities, so you'll keep the kitchen stocked but the vegetable garden will not become an unending chore.

The garden in summer can be an extra living room where family and guests spill outside. Design garden spaces to invite evening walks, or build a patio where you can serve friends after-dinner coffee. A terrace, close to the kitchen, equipped with a barbecue and a table makes eating meals outside fun and easy.

SUMMER

DATE: _____

TEMPERATURE A.M.: _____

WEATHER BRIEFS: _____

_____

_____

COLOR IN THE GARDEN: _____

_____

_____

SPECIAL PLEASURES: _____

_____

LESSONS LEARNED: _____

_____

TRIUMPHS: _____

_____

DON'T FORGET: _____

_____

PLAN AHEAD: _____

_____

NOTES: _____

TEMPERATURE P.M.: _____

GARDEN VISITORS *(birds, insects, critters)*: _____

_____

_____

_____

_____

_____

_____

_____

_____

_____

_____

_____

_____

DATE: _____

TEMPERATURE A.M.: _____

TEMPERATURE P.M.: _____

WEATHER BRIEFS: _____

GARDEN VISITORS *(birds, insects, critters)*: ____

_____

_____

_____

COLOR IN THE GARDEN: _____

_____

_____

_____

_____

_____

SPECIAL PLEASURES: _____

_____

LESSONS LEARNED: _____

_____

TRIUMPHS: _____

_____

DON'T FORGET: _____

_____

PLAN AHEAD: _____

_____

NOTES: _____

_____

_____

_____

_____

_____

SUMMER

DATE:

TEMPERATURE A.M.:

TEMPERATURE P.M.:

WEATHER BRIEFS:

GARDEN VISITORS *(birds, insects, critters)*:

COLOR IN THE GARDEN:

SPECIAL PLEASURES:

LESSONS LEARNED:

TRIUMPHS:

DON'T FORGET:

PLAN AHEAD:

NOTES:

SUMMER

DATE:

TEMPERATURE A.M.:

TEMPERATURE P.M.:

WEATHER BRIEFS:

GARDEN VISITORS *(birds, insects, critters)*:

COLOR IN THE GARDEN:

SPECIAL PLEASURES:

LESSONS LEARNED:

TRIUMPHS:

DON'T FORGET:

PLAN AHEAD:

NOTES:

GRILL SUMMER VEGETABLES

Firing up the grill as the heat of the day fades and the evening breeze stirs is a summer tradition. The grill may be crowded with hamburgers, chicken breasts, or steaks, but push them aside to make room for grilled vegetables. Brush olive oil on sliced zucchinis; skewer cherry tomatoes; or add whole peppers, small onions, or corn on the cob. Grill the vegetables just until tender; cook the cherry tomatoes very briefly, or they will fall off the skewers. Grilled vegetables are a revelation, and even the most antivegetable set—usually aged under ten—will appreciate these flavor-packed treats.

STAGE A TOMATO TASTING

Tomatoes are the cult figures of the summer garden, and they are a focal point of discussion among enthusiasts in many neighborhoods and community gardens. If you have several friends or neighbors who love tomatoes, you can create an annual summer event by collectively choosing varieties of tomatoes to grow, distributing seeds or plants, and then arranging a tasting of each gardener's tomatoes. These plants are particularly sensitive to microclimates, fertilizing techniques, and soils, and the various results may astonish all the participants.

SUMMER

DATE:

TEMPERATURE A.M.: | TEMPERATURE P.M.:

WEATHER BRIEFS: | GARDEN VISITORS *(birds, insects, critters)*:

COLOR IN THE GARDEN:

SPECIAL PLEASURES:

LESSONS LEARNED:

TRIUMPHS:

DON'T FORGET:

PLAN AHEAD:

NOTES:

SUMMER

DATE:

TEMPERATURE A.M.: _____

TEMPERATURE P.M.: _____

WEATHER BRIEFS: _____

_____

_____

COLOR IN THE GARDEN: _____

_____

_____

GARDEN VISITORS *(birds, insects, critters)*: _____

_____

_____

_____

_____

SPECIAL PLEASURES: _____

_____

LESSONS LEARNED: _____

_____

TRIUMPHS: _____

_____

DON'T FORGET: _____

_____

PLAN AHEAD: _____

_____

NOTES: _____

_____

_____

_____

_____

_____

SUMMER

DATE:

TEMPERATURE A.M.:

TEMPERATURE P.M.:

WEATHER BRIEFS:

GARDEN VISITORS *(birds, insects, critters)*:

COLOR IN THE GARDEN:

SPECIAL PLEASURES:

LESSONS LEARNED:

TRIUMPHS:

DON'T FORGET:

PLAN AHEAD:

NOTES:

SUMMER

DATE: _____

TEMPERATURE A.M.: _____   TEMPERATURE P.M.: _____

WEATHER BRIEFS: _____   GARDEN VISITORS *(birds, insects, critters)*:

_____   _____

_____   _____

COLOR IN THE GARDEN: _____   _____

_____   _____

_____   _____

SPECIAL PLEASURES: _____

_____

LESSONS LEARNED: _____

_____

TRIUMPHS: _____

_____

DON'T FORGET: _____

_____

PLAN AHEAD: _____

_____

NOTES: _____

_____

_____

_____

_____

_____

SUMMER

DATE:

TEMPERATURE A.M.: _____

TEMPERATURE P.M.: _____

WEATHER BRIEFS: _____

GARDEN VISITORS *(birds, insects, critters)*: _____

COLOR IN THE GARDEN: _____

SPECIAL PLEASURES: _____

LESSONS LEARNED: _____

TRIUMPHS: _____

DON'T FORGET: _____

PLAN AHEAD: _____

NOTES: _____

QUICK ADDITIONS
TO THE PANTRY

1. When you are short of time, with too many tomatoes begging to be harvested, pick them, place them whole in a Ziploc freezer bag, and freeze. When you are ready to cook with them, thaw, slip off the skins, and use the tomatoes in soups, stews, or sauce.

2. Everyone loves basil pesto, but you can replace the basil with parsley, cilantro, or even mint.

3. Dried herbs always come in handy in a pantry. Clip large quantities of herbs, such as sage, marjoram, and rosemary, bind them together or separately in hanks with kitchen twine, and hang them in a warm place protected from morning dews. When crisp, place the herbs in jars, leaving the leaves as whole as possible, and store them in a cool, dark place. Just before using, break up the leaves. Storing the leaves whole preserves their flavor, and breaking them up for cooking releases that flavor. Renew your herb pantry every year.

SUMMER

DATE: _____

TEMPERATURE A.M.: _____　　TEMPERATURE P.M.: _____

WEATHER BRIEFS: _____　　GARDEN VISITORS *(birds, insects, critters)*:

_____　　_____

_____　　_____

COLOR IN THE GARDEN: _____　　_____

_____　　_____

_____　　_____

SPECIAL PLEASURES: _____

_____

LESSONS LEARNED: _____

_____

TRIUMPHS: _____

_____

DON'T FORGET: _____

_____

PLAN AHEAD: _____

_____

NOTES: _____

_____

_____

_____

_____

_____

TEMPERATURE A.M.: _____

TEMPERATURE P.M.: _____

WEATHER BRIEFS: _____

GARDEN VISITORS *(birds, insects, critters)*:

_____

COLOR IN THE GARDEN: _____

_____

SPECIAL PLEASURES: _____

LESSONS LEARNED: _____

TRIUMPHS: _____

DON'T FORGET: _____

PLAN AHEAD: _____

NOTES: _____

_____

SUMMER

DATE:

TEMPERATURE A.M.: _____

TEMPERATURE P.M.: _____

WEATHER BRIEFS: _____

GARDEN VISITORS *(birds, insects, critters)*: _____

_____

_____

COLOR IN THE GARDEN: _____

_____

_____

SPECIAL PLEASURES: _____

LESSONS LEARNED: _____

TRIUMPHS: _____

DON'T FORGET: _____

PLAN AHEAD: _____

NOTES: _____

_____

_____

_____

_____

_____

SUMMER

DATE: _____

TEMPERATURE A.M.: _____

TEMPERATURE P.M.: _____

WEATHER BRIEFS: _____

GARDEN VISITORS *(birds, insects, critters)*: _____

_____

_____

COLOR IN THE GARDEN: _____

_____

_____

SPECIAL PLEASURES: _____

LESSONS LEARNED: _____

TRIUMPHS: _____

DON'T FORGET: _____

PLAN AHEAD: _____

NOTES: _____

_____

_____

_____

_____

TEMPERATURE A.M.:

TEMPERATURE P.M.:

WEATHER BRIEFS:

GARDEN VISITORS *(birds, insects, critters)*:

COLOR IN THE GARDEN:

SPECIAL PLEASURES:

LESSONS LEARNED:

TRIUMPHS:

DON'T FORGET:

PLAN AHEAD:

NOTES:

SUMMER

DATE: _____

TEMPERATURE A.M.: _____

TEMPERATURE P.M.: _____

WEATHER BRIEFS: _____

GARDEN VISITORS *(birds, insects, critters)*: _____

_____

_____

COLOR IN THE GARDEN: _____

_____

_____

SPECIAL PLEASURES: _____

_____

LESSONS LEARNED: _____

_____

TRIUMPHS: _____

_____

DON'T FORGET: _____

_____

PLAN AHEAD: _____

_____

NOTES: _____

_____

_____

_____

_____

_____

SUMMER

DATE:

TEMPERATURE A.M.:

TEMPERATURE P.M.:

WEATHER BRIEFS:

GARDEN VISITORS *(birds, insects, critters)*:

COLOR IN THE GARDEN:

SPECIAL PLEASURES:

LESSONS LEARNED:

TRIUMPHS:

DON'T FORGET:

PLAN AHEAD:

NOTES:

CHOOSE PLANTS THAT
ATTRACT BENEFICIAL INSECTS

Beneficial insects either prey on all manner of insects that love to share the garden's harvest or work as busy pollinators, thereby increasing the harvest. Nectar plants and bee pollen plants issue a siren's call and fill your garden with insects that can assist you. Try to plant some of the following bug magnets in both your vegetable and flower gardens:

BORAGE
The flowers' nectar is beloved by bees. (Annual)

COSMOS
Pink and white blossoms attract various bugs. (Annual)

LAVENDER
Bees and bumblebees will come to sample. (Perennial)

NEPETA
These are easy-to-grow bug magnets. (Perennial)

SAGE
All common varieties attract nectar-loving insects. (Perennial)

SUNFLOWERS
These are both fun to grow and attract a variety of good bugs.
(Annual)

SUMMER

DATE: _____

TEMPERATURE A.M.: _____

WEATHER BRIEFS: _____

COLOR IN THE GARDEN: _____

TEMPERATURE P.M.: _____

GARDEN VISITORS *(birds, insects, critters)*: _____

SPECIAL PLEASURES: _____

LESSONS LEARNED: _____

TRIUMPHS: _____

DON'T FORGET: _____

PLAN AHEAD: _____

NOTES: _____

TEMPERATURE A.M.:

TEMPERATURE P.M.:

WEATHER BRIEFS:

GARDEN VISITORS *(birds, insects, critters)*:

COLOR IN THE GARDEN:

SPECIAL PLEASURES:

LESSONS LEARNED:

TRIUMPHS:

DON'T FORGET:

PLAN AHEAD:

NOTES:

SUMMER

DATE: _____

TEMPERATURE A.M.: _____

TEMPERATURE P.M.: _____

WEATHER BRIEFS: _____

GARDEN VISITORS *(birds, insects, critters)*: _____

_____

_____

COLOR IN THE GARDEN: _____

_____

_____

SPECIAL PLEASURES: _____

LESSONS LEARNED: _____

TRIUMPHS: _____

DON'T FORGET: _____

PLAN AHEAD: _____

NOTES: _____

_____

_____

_____

_____

SUMMER

DATE:

TEMPERATURE A.M.:

TEMPERATURE P.M.:

WEATHER BRIEFS:

GARDEN VISITORS *(birds, insects, critters)*:

COLOR IN THE GARDEN:

SPECIAL PLEASURES:

LESSONS LEARNED:

TRIUMPHS:

DON'T FORGET:

PLAN AHEAD:

NOTES:

TEMPERATURE A.M.:   TEMPERATURE P.M.:

WEATHER BRIEFS: GARDEN VISITORS *(birds, insects, critters)*:

COLOR IN THE GARDEN:

SPECIAL PLEASURES:

LESSONS LEARNED:

TRIUMPHS:

DON'T FORGET:

PLAN AHEAD:

NOTES:

SUMMER

DATE: _____

TEMPERATURE A.M.: _____

WEATHER BRIEFS: _____

_____

_____

COLOR IN THE GARDEN: _____

_____

_____

SPECIAL PLEASURES: _____

_____

LESSONS LEARNED: _____

_____

TRIUMPHS: _____

_____

DON'T FORGET: _____

_____

PLAN AHEAD: _____

_____

NOTES: _____

_____

_____

_____

_____

_____

TEMPERATURE P.M.: _____

GARDEN VISITORS *(birds, insects, critters)*:

_____

_____

_____

_____

_____

_____

_____

_____

SUMMER

DATE:

TEMPERATURE A.M.: _____

TEMPERATURE P.M.: _____

WEATHER BRIEFS: _____

GARDEN VISITORS *(birds, insects, critters)*:

COLOR IN THE GARDEN: _____

SPECIAL PLEASURES: _____

LESSONS LEARNED: _____

TRIUMPHS: _____

DON'T FORGET: _____

PLAN AHEAD: _____

NOTES: _____

PINCH BACK
CHRYSANTHEMUMS

There is an old adage that applies throughout the United States: "Six inches high by the Fourth of July." This handy phrase means that you need to keep pinching back your chrysanthemums to a height of 6 inches until July 4. Add some staking to support the mature flowers.

STAKE CLIMBING PLANTS

When planting climbing vines, whether beans, cucumbers, melons, tomatoes, or flowering plants, set up the staking even before you water the newly established plants. Large tomato hoops—avoid the small, wimpy variety—work well for a variety of climbing plants, and you can add height by weaving in sticks that stretch above the hoops. Concrete reinforcing wire circled in 5-foot-diameter rounds makes grand climbing support, and its 6-inch-wide squares make reaching in to pick tomatoes or other vegetables easy. No matter what the staking system, be sure to install it at the time of planting.

SUMMER

DATE:

TEMPERATURE A.M.:   TEMPERATURE P.M.:

WEATHER BRIEFS: GARDEN VISITORS *(birds, insects, critters)*:

COLOR IN THE GARDEN:

SPECIAL PLEASURES:

LESSONS LEARNED:

TRIUMPHS:

DON'T FORGET:

PLAN AHEAD:

NOTES:

SUMMER

DATE:

TEMPERATURE A.M.:

TEMPERATURE P.M.:

WEATHER BRIEFS:

GARDEN VISITORS *(birds, insects, critters)*:

COLOR IN THE GARDEN:

SPECIAL PLEASURES:

LESSONS LEARNED:

TRIUMPHS:

DON'T FORGET:

PLAN AHEAD:

NOTES:

SUMMER

DATE:

TEMPERATURE A.M.: _____

TEMPERATURE P.M.: _____

WEATHER BRIEFS: _____

GARDEN VISITORS *(birds, insects, critters)*: _____

_____

_____

_____

_____

COLOR IN THE GARDEN: _____

_____

_____

_____

_____

SPECIAL PLEASURES: _____

_____

LESSONS LEARNED: _____

_____

TRIUMPHS: _____

_____

DON'T FORGET: _____

_____

PLAN AHEAD: _____

_____

NOTES: _____

_____

_____

_____

_____

_____

TEMPERATURE A.M.:

TEMPERATURE P.M.:

WEATHER BRIEFS:

GARDEN VISITORS *(birds, insects, critters)*:

COLOR IN THE GARDEN:

SPECIAL PLEASURES:

LESSONS LEARNED:

TRIUMPHS:

DON'T FORGET:

PLAN AHEAD:

NOTES:

TEMPERATURE A.M.:   TEMPERATURE P.M.:

WEATHER BRIEFS: GARDEN VISITORS *(birds, insects, critters)*:

COLOR IN THE GARDEN:

SPECIAL PLEASURES:

LESSONS LEARNED:

TRIUMPHS:

DON'T FORGET:

PLAN AHEAD:

NOTES:

SUMMER

DATE: _____

TEMPERATURE A.M.: _____   TEMPERATURE P.M.: _____

WEATHER BRIEFS: _____   GARDEN VISITORS *(birds, insects, critters)*:

_____   _____

_____   _____

COLOR IN THE GARDEN: _____   _____

_____   _____

_____   _____

SPECIAL PLEASURES: _____

_____

LESSONS LEARNED: _____

_____

TRIUMPHS: _____

_____

DON'T FORGET: _____

_____

PLAN AHEAD: _____

_____

NOTES: _____

_____

_____

_____

_____

_____

LET MULCH
WORK FOR YOU

Mulch is one of the gardener's best tools for saving water and keeping weeds under control and plants happy. Mulch, a layer of "green" insulation added to the soil, keeps soil temperatures constant, seals in moisture, and inhibits weeds. Straw, compost, dried grass clippings, and wood chips are good materials for mulch. Add a 3- to 4-inch layer of mulch around the stems of young vegetables once the ground has warmed up in summer. Mulch perennial flower beds early in the spring, first with newspaper and then with a thick covering of mulch, for the best weed protection.

SUMMER

DATE:

TEMPERATURE A.M.:   TEMPERATURE P.M.:

WEATHER BRIEFS: GARDEN VISITORS *(birds, insects, critters)*:

COLOR IN THE GARDEN:

SPECIAL PLEASURES:

LESSONS LEARNED:

TRIUMPHS:

DON'T FORGET:

PLAN AHEAD:

NOTES:

SUMMER

DATE: _____

TEMPERATURE A.M.: _____

TEMPERATURE P.M.: _____

WEATHER BRIEFS: _____

GARDEN VISITORS *(birds, insects, critters)*: _____

COLOR IN THE GARDEN: _____

SPECIAL PLEASURES: _____

LESSONS LEARNED: _____

TRIUMPHS: _____

DON'T FORGET: _____

PLAN AHEAD: _____

NOTES: _____

SUMMER

DATE:

TEMPERATURE A.M.:

TEMPERATURE P.M.:

WEATHER BRIEFS:

GARDEN VISITORS *(birds, insects, critters)*:

COLOR IN THE GARDEN:

SPECIAL PLEASURES:

LESSONS LEARNED:

TRIUMPHS:

DON'T FORGET:

PLAN AHEAD:

NOTES:

SUMMER

DATE:

TEMPERATURE A.M.:

TEMPERATURE P.M.:

WEATHER BRIEFS:

GARDEN VISITORS *(birds, insects, critters)*:

COLOR IN THE GARDEN:

SPECIAL PLEASURES:

LESSONS LEARNED:

TRIUMPHS:

DON'T FORGET:

PLAN AHEAD:

NOTES:

SUMMER

DATE:

TEMPERATURE A.M.:

TEMPERATURE P.M.:

WEATHER BRIEFS:

GARDEN VISITORS *(birds, insects, critters)*:

COLOR IN THE GARDEN:

SPECIAL PLEASURES:

LESSONS LEARNED:

TRIUMPHS:

DON'T FORGET:

PLAN AHEAD:

NOTES:

Gardener's Summer
CHECKLIST

○ Sow any remaining annual flower seeds and the last of the summer vegetable seedlings.

○ Keep up with the weeding and spread 2 to 3 inches of mulch around perennials, shrubs, and trees to limit future problems.

○ Check to make sure climbing vines have reached their support structures. Use garden twine as guide wires to assist tendrils upwards.

○ Deadhead late-spring-blooming bulbs but do not cut off foliage until it has yellowed and withered. Prune off late-spring shrub blooms.

○ Harvest garlic and onions when bulbs reach mature size and the foliage begins to yellow and fall over.

○ Order spring-blooming bulbs for fall planting.

○ During heat spells, water roses deeply. Fertilize monthly for maximum bloom.

○ Pinch back chrysanthemums to 6 inches high until July 4.

○ Irrigate during dry spells and make sure to check all irrigation hoses for leaks and clogged lines.

○ Prop up heavily laden fruit tree branches that could break.

○ In late summer, clean out spent vegetable beds, fertilize, add compost, and set in cool-season vegetables for your fall and winter garden.

○ Photograph garden beds at the height of their bloom.

○ Check iris clumps during bloom and note which ones will need dividing in the fall.

○ Fertilize asparagus beds when harvest ends.

○ Check irrigation hoses for leaks and clogged lines and start to irrigate during dry spells.

○ When apples are quarter-sized, thin them to one per spur.

○ Prop up heavily laden fruit tree branches that could break.

○ Deadhead roses and fertilize them for the second flush of bloom.

○ Plant a row of ornamental sunflowers for summer bouquets.

○ Pinch back chrysanthemums to 6 inches high until July 4.

○ Keep ivy or other ground covers under control with constant pruning.

○ Keep up with the weeding and spread 2 to 3 inches of mulch around perennials, shrubs, and trees to limit future problems.

○ When catalogs arrive, order spring-flowering bulbs for fall planting.

○ Buy seeds of cool-season vegetables and sow them in late summer, when early-summer vegetables are spent. Renew beds with fertilizer and compost before planting.

○ Photograph garden beds on the summer equinox.

- When catalogs arrive, order spring-flowering bulbs for fall planting.

- Prop up heavily laden fruit tree branches that could break.

- Deadhead summer-blooming bulbs.

- Mulch beds deeply to protect plants from the hottest weather.

- In late summer, sow seeds indoors for winter vegetables such as cabbages, broccoli, kale, and chard.

- Check watering systems for breaks and leaks. Water flower and vegetable beds deeply early in the morning.

- Move containers that suffer from heat stress into partial shade. Fertilize and make sure they receive adequate amounts of water.

- Trim blooming herbs to dry for herb blends.

- Take out spent plants and replace with fall-blooming annuals. Keep watered.

- Photograph garden beds at the height of their bloom.

○ Hang pheromone traps in apple trees at bud break, and after June drop, when the tree naturally sheds some of the excess apples, thin apple clusters to one apple per spur.

○ Sow any remaining annual flower seeds and the last of the summer vegetable seedlings.

○ Harvest garlic and onions when bulbs reach mature size and the foliage begins to yellow and fall over.

○ Check irrigation hoses for leaks and clogged lines and start to irrigate during dry spells.

○ Prop up heavily laden fruit tree branches that could break.

○ Plant a row of ornamental sunflowers for summer bouquets.

○ Deadhead summer annuals to encourage continued bloom.

○ Deadhead roses and fertilize them for the second flush of bloom. Prune back climbing roses after bloom.

○ Check iris clumps during bloom and note which ones will need dividing in the fall.

○ Pinch back chrysanthemums to 6 inches high until July 4.

GARDEN SKETCHES

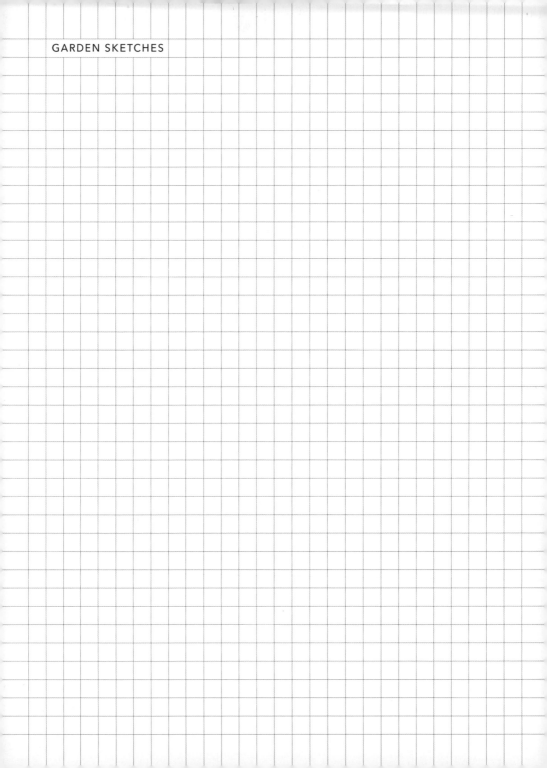

GARDEN SKETCHES

GARDEN SKETCHES

FALL

Fall slides into the garden in a quiet manner. Suddenly nighttime temperatures drop several degrees, and you reach for a jacket to cut the chill of early morning.

SHADOWS begin to lengthen, leaves to drop—perhaps only just a few here and a few there—and the light changes, too. The garden slows to a halt, looking suddenly blowsy and overblown.

Fall, with its aptly falling leaves and forming seedpods, signals the end of the growing season. Your garden time now will be spent harvesting, tidying up, raking leaves, cutting back, and putting away. Fall seems like the cleanup after a glorious party. Pumpkins and winter squash must be harvested and put into winter storage. The last ripe tomatoes need to be picked and made into sauce or canned, or they can be savored in the last homegrown BLT. You can sour-pickle green tomatoes or make them into sweet mincemeat with raisins and cinnamon, perfect for Thanksgiving pies.

If there is any basil left in the garden, this is the last time to make pesto, frozen or canned, to ladle over pasta during the next six months. Fill empty wine bottles with cider vinegar and herbs to store up summer's flavors. Plug in your dehydrator, if you have one, to dry thyme, tarragon, summer savory, and rosemary for a flavorful herb blend, or hyssop, rose hips, and mint for herbal teas. Spent plants need to be pulled out. Time is running out—soon frost will close the garden for the year.

In the ornamental garden, you must also make haste to get tender plants into protected spaces: place frost-tender bulbs and deciduous plants under eaves or in sun porches, cellars, or garages. In snow-cold areas in late fall, plants susceptible to cold must be heavily mulched with straw or surrounded with burlap to survive the coming snow and low temperatures.

Take time to sum up your garden's growing year, writing down your successes and, of course, as in every garden, your failures, as well as goals reached or not yet attained.

FALL

DATE: _____

TEMPERATURE A.M.: _____

TEMPERATURE P.M.: _____

WEATHER BRIEFS: _____

GARDEN VISITORS *(birds, insects, critters)*: _____

_____

_____

_____

COLOR IN THE GARDEN: _____

_____

_____

_____

_____

SPECIAL PLEASURES: _____

_____

LESSONS LEARNED: _____

_____

TRIUMPHS: _____

_____

DON'T FORGET: _____

_____

PLAN AHEAD: _____

_____

NOTES: _____

_____

_____

_____

_____

_____

FALL

DATE: _____

TEMPERATURE A.M.: _____

WEATHER BRIEFS: _____

_____

_____

COLOR IN THE GARDEN: _____

_____

_____

SPECIAL PLEASURES: _____

_____

LESSONS LEARNED: _____

_____

TRIUMPHS: _____

_____

DON'T FORGET: _____

_____

PLAN AHEAD: _____

_____

NOTES: _____

_____

_____

_____

_____

TEMPERATURE P.M.: _____

GARDEN VISITORS *(birds, insects, critters)*: _____

_____

_____

_____

_____

_____

FALL

DATE:

TEMPERATURE A.M.:   TEMPERATURE P.M.:

WEATHER BRIEFS: GARDEN VISITORS *(birds, insects, critters)*:

COLOR IN THE GARDEN:

SPECIAL PLEASURES:

LESSONS LEARNED:

TRIUMPHS:

DON'T FORGET:

PLAN AHEAD:

NOTES:

FALL

TEMPERATURE A.M.:

TEMPERATURE P.M.:

WEATHER BRIEFS:

GARDEN VISITORS *(birds, insects, critters)*:

COLOR IN THE GARDEN:

SPECIAL PLEASURES:

LESSONS LEARNED:

TRIUMPHS:

DON'T FORGET:

PLAN AHEAD:

NOTES:

DATE:

TEMPERATURE A.M.:

TEMPERATURE P.M.:

WEATHER BRIEFS:

GARDEN VISITORS *(birds, insects, critters)*:

COLOR IN THE GARDEN:

SPECIAL PLEASURES:

LESSONS LEARNED:

TRIUMPHS:

DON'T FORGET:

PLAN AHEAD:

NOTES:

FALL

DATE:

TEMPERATURE A.M.: _____

TEMPERATURE P.M.: _____

WEATHER BRIEFS: _____

GARDEN VISITORS *(birds, insects, critters)*:

_____

_____

COLOR IN THE GARDEN: _____

_____

_____

SPECIAL PLEASURES: _____

LESSONS LEARNED: _____

TRIUMPHS: _____

DON'T FORGET: _____

PLAN AHEAD: _____

NOTES: _____

_____

_____

_____

_____

_____

BUY SPRING BULBS

If you didn't buy them earlier in the year, shop for spring-blooming bulbs, either through catalogs or at stores and nurseries. Because bulbs are both seasonal and perishable, businesses stock only limited amounts, and the choice bulbs sell out quickly. When buying daffodils, look for bulbs with multiple parts, called noses. Each nose will bear a bloom stalk. With all types of bulbs, pick out fat, plump specimens and avoid any that are shriveled or show soft, mushy spots. When planting, dig a hole twice as deep as the bulb's height. If you can't tell the top of the bulb from its bottom, plant the bulb sideways. Try to plant your bulbs before the first frost if possible.

TO PLAN AHEAD, LOOK BACK

Make a note of the last flowers blooming in your garden, and take the time to jot down the date when your deciduous shrubs and trees lose their leaves. These notes will allow you to choose later-blooming flowers and shrubs that will extend the beauty of your garden in coming years. Make sure to note the date of the first frost every year, as that alert will allow you to protect tender plants and sensitive bulbs from dropping temperatures next time fall rolls around.

FALL

DATE:

TEMPERATURE A.M.: _____   TEMPERATURE P.M.: _____

WEATHER BRIEFS: _____   GARDEN VISITORS *(birds, insects, critters)*:

_____   _____

_____   _____

COLOR IN THE GARDEN: _____   _____

_____   _____

_____   _____

SPECIAL PLEASURES: _____

_____

LESSONS LEARNED: _____

_____

TRIUMPHS: _____

_____

DON'T FORGET: _____

_____

PLAN AHEAD: _____

_____

NOTES: _____

_____

_____

_____

_____

_____

FALL

DATE: _____

TEMPERATURE A.M.: _____

WEATHER BRIEFS:

_____

_____

COLOR IN THE GARDEN:

_____

_____

SPECIAL PLEASURES:

_____

LESSONS LEARNED:

_____

TRIUMPHS:

_____

DON'T FORGET:

_____

PLAN AHEAD:

_____

NOTES:

_____

_____

_____

_____

_____

TEMPERATURE P.M.: _____

GARDEN VISITORS *(birds, insects, critters)*:

_____

_____

_____

_____

_____

FALL

DATE:

TEMPERATURE A.M.:   TEMPERATURE P.M.:

WEATHER BRIEFS: GARDEN VISITORS *(birds, insects, critters)*:

COLOR IN THE GARDEN:

SPECIAL PLEASURES:

LESSONS LEARNED:

TRIUMPHS:

DON'T FORGET:

PLAN AHEAD:

NOTES:

FALL

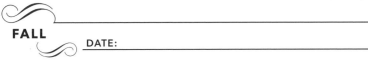

DATE:

TEMPERATURE A.M.:

TEMPERATURE P.M.:

WEATHER BRIEFS:

GARDEN VISITORS *(birds, insects, critters)*:

COLOR IN THE GARDEN:

SPECIAL PLEASURES:

LESSONS LEARNED:

TRIUMPHS:

DON'T FORGET:

PLAN AHEAD:

NOTES:

FALL

DATE: _____

TEMPERATURE A.M.: _____

TEMPERATURE P.M.: _____

WEATHER BRIEFS: _____

GARDEN VISITORS *(birds, insects, critters)*:

_____

_____

COLOR IN THE GARDEN: _____

_____

_____

_____

_____

SPECIAL PLEASURES: _____

_____

LESSONS LEARNED: _____

_____

TRIUMPHS: _____

_____

DON'T FORGET: _____

_____

PLAN AHEAD: _____

_____

NOTES: _____

_____

_____

_____

_____

_____

FALL

DATE:

TEMPERATURE A.M.:

TEMPERATURE P.M.:

WEATHER BRIEFS:

GARDEN VISITORS *(birds, insects, critters)*:

COLOR IN THE GARDEN:

SPECIAL PLEASURES:

LESSONS LEARNED:

TRIUMPHS:

DON'T FORGET:

PLAN AHEAD:

NOTES:

HARVEST WINTER
SQUASH AND PUMPKINS

Although they can be eaten when small, acorn, butternut, and buttercup squash are best left to mature so they can produce meat with rich texture and flavor. Leave the fruits on the vine until their skin is too hard to be pierced by your fingernail. When harvesting, leave about 2 to 3 inches of stem on the squash to avoid rot. Store squash and pumpkins in a dark place at a temperature of about 50°F. A box in a closet in a cool room works well if you don't have a harvest room or root cellar.

FALL

DATE:

TEMPERATURE A.M.: _____

TEMPERATURE P.M.: _____

WEATHER BRIEFS: _____

GARDEN VISITORS *(birds, insects, critters)*: _____

_____

_____

COLOR IN THE GARDEN: _____

_____

_____

SPECIAL PLEASURES: _____

LESSONS LEARNED: _____

TRIUMPHS: _____

DON'T FORGET: _____

PLAN AHEAD: _____

NOTES: _____

_____

_____

_____

_____

FALL

DATE:

TEMPERATURE A.M.: _____

TEMPERATURE P.M.: _____

WEATHER BRIEFS: _____

GARDEN VISITORS *(birds, insects, critters)*: _____

_____

_____

_____

_____

COLOR IN THE GARDEN: _____

_____

_____

_____

_____

_____

SPECIAL PLEASURES: _____

_____

LESSONS LEARNED: _____

_____

TRIUMPHS: _____

_____

DON'T FORGET: _____

_____

PLAN AHEAD: _____

_____

NOTES: _____

_____

_____

_____

_____

_____

_____

_____

FALL

DATE:

TEMPERATURE A.M.:

TEMPERATURE P.M.:

WEATHER BRIEFS:

GARDEN VISITORS *(birds, insects, critters)*:

COLOR IN THE GARDEN:

SPECIAL PLEASURES:

LESSONS LEARNED:

TRIUMPHS:

DON'T FORGET:

PLAN AHEAD:

NOTES:

DATE:

TEMPERATURE A.M.:

TEMPERATURE P.M.:

WEATHER BRIEFS:

GARDEN VISITORS *(birds, insects, critters)*:

COLOR IN THE GARDEN:

SPECIAL PLEASURES:

LESSONS LEARNED:

TRIUMPHS:

DON'T FORGET:

PLAN AHEAD:

NOTES:

FALL

DATE:

TEMPERATURE A.M.: _____

TEMPERATURE P.M.: _____

WEATHER BRIEFS: _____

GARDEN VISITORS *(birds, insects, critters)*: _____

COLOR IN THE GARDEN: _____

SPECIAL PLEASURES: _____

LESSONS LEARNED: _____

TRIUMPHS: _____

DON'T FORGET: _____

PLAN AHEAD: _____

NOTES: _____

FALL

DATE:

TEMPERATURE A.M.: _____

TEMPERATURE P.M.: _____

WEATHER BRIEFS: _____

GARDEN VISITORS *(birds, insects, critters)*: _____

_____

_____

_____

_____

COLOR IN THE GARDEN: _____

_____

_____

_____

_____

SPECIAL PLEASURES: _____

_____

LESSONS LEARNED: _____

_____

TRIUMPHS: _____

_____

DON'T FORGET: _____

_____

PLAN AHEAD: _____

_____

NOTES: _____

_____

_____

_____

_____

_____

TEMPERATURE A.M.:

TEMPERATURE P.M.:

WEATHER BRIEFS:

GARDEN VISITORS *(birds, insects, critters)*:

COLOR IN THE GARDEN:

SPECIAL PLEASURES:

LESSONS LEARNED:

TRIUMPHS:

DON'T FORGET:

PLAN AHEAD:

NOTES:

PICK ROSE HIPS
FOR TEA

Many varieties of roses produce hips, or seed pods that form after bloom. Rugosa roses are renowned for their hips, which appear on the bush as large, spectacularly bright orange-red berries after the blooms have finished, a two-for-one display. Clip off these hips with shears or scissors, dry them thoroughly on a plate in a warm place until they harden, and store them in a glass container with your herbs in a cool, dark place. For a tart-tasting tea filled with vitamin C, cover the hips with boiling water. Remember, if you deadhead your roses, you won't get any hips.

FALL   DATE:

TEMPERATURE A.M.:

TEMPERATURE P.M.:

WEATHER BRIEFS:

GARDEN VISITORS *(birds, insects, critters)*:

COLOR IN THE GARDEN:

SPECIAL PLEASURES:

LESSONS LEARNED:

TRIUMPHS:

DON'T FORGET:

PLAN AHEAD:

NOTES:

FALL

DATE:

TEMPERATURE A.M.: _____

TEMPERATURE P.M.: _____

WEATHER BRIEFS: _____

GARDEN VISITORS *(birds, insects, critters)*: _____

COLOR IN THE GARDEN: _____

SPECIAL PLEASURES: _____

LESSONS LEARNED: _____

TRIUMPHS: _____

DON'T FORGET: _____

PLAN AHEAD: _____

NOTES: _____

FALL

DATE: _____

TEMPERATURE A.M.: _____　　TEMPERATURE P.M.: _____

WEATHER BRIEFS: _____

GARDEN VISITORS *(birds, insects, critters)*: _____

_____

_____

COLOR IN THE GARDEN: _____

_____

_____

_____

SPECIAL PLEASURES: _____

LESSONS LEARNED: _____

TRIUMPHS: _____

DON'T FORGET: _____

PLAN AHEAD: _____

NOTES: _____

_____

_____

_____

_____

_____

TEMPERATURE A.M.:

TEMPERATURE P.M.:

WEATHER BRIEFS:

GARDEN VISITORS *(birds, insects, critters)*:

COLOR IN THE GARDEN:

SPECIAL PLEASURES:

LESSONS LEARNED:

TRIUMPHS:

DON'T FORGET:

PLAN AHEAD:

NOTES:

DATE:

TEMPERATURE A.M.:

TEMPERATURE P.M.:

WEATHER BRIEFS:

GARDEN VISITORS *(birds, insects, critters)*:

COLOR IN THE GARDEN:

SPECIAL PLEASURES:

LESSONS LEARNED:

TRIUMPHS:

DON'T FORGET:

PLAN AHEAD:

NOTES:

SAVE HEIRLOOM
TOMATO SEEDS

Saving seeds from your own heirloom tomatoes has a distinct advantage. Plants grown for several seasons in the same place adapt to their home garden, which increases their ability to flourish in their particular microclimate and garden soil.

To start, select tomatoes from the best plants—those that seem the most vigorous and healthy—picking out the largest, ripest fruits to save. Because each plant has a slightly different genetic code, pick tomatoes from three or more plants of the same variety if possible.

The seeds must go through a fermentation process to destroy any diseases they carry. As the seeds ferment, microorganisms cleanse them of diseases that could affect next year's plants.

Slice open the fruit and scoop the seeds in their gel sack into a glass or container labeled with the variety's name. Fill the containers half full of room-temperature water. Any seeds that float are not viable, so skim them off. Let the containers sit uncovered at room temperature until the water's surface is partially covered with white mold; this takes about three to five days, depending upon the specific temperature. Slip off the white mold and discard it, saving the seeds. Refill the container with clean, room-temperature water and stir. Pour off any floating pulp, again making sure not to discard the seeds. Then, in a fine sieve, drain the seeds as thoroughly as possible, using a paper tower to wipe dry the bottom of the sieve. Turn the seeds out onto a labeled ceramic, glass, or metal dish—not one made of paper, which will stick tenaciously to the drying seeds.

Dry the seeds in a warm place out of direct sun, but never in a location above 96°F, because the seeds die at high temperatures. When the seeds are thoroughly dry, store them in glass jars or glassine envelopes labeled with the source of the plant (catalog, neighbor, nursery, or garage sale), the variety name, and the date and location the seeds were collected. Keeping the seeds dry discourages fungal diseases and conditions that may cause the seeds to prematurely sprout. In the spring, 6 to 8 weeks before the last frost, plant your seeds indoors in containers, lightly covering them with soil and keeping them moist. Seeds will sprout quickly and easily within 5 to 10 days. Seeds stored properly may last for several years, but the most reliable germination is the next planting season.

FALL

DATE: _____

TEMPERATURE A.M.: _____

TEMPERATURE P.M.: _____

WEATHER BRIEFS: _____

GARDEN VISITORS *(birds, insects, critters)*: _____

_____

_____

_____

_____

COLOR IN THE GARDEN: _____

_____

_____

_____

_____

SPECIAL PLEASURES: _____

_____

LESSONS LEARNED: _____

_____

TRIUMPHS: _____

_____

DON'T FORGET: _____

_____

PLAN AHEAD: _____

_____

NOTES: _____

_____

_____

_____

_____

_____

FALL

DATE:

TEMPERATURE A.M.:

TEMPERATURE P.M.:

WEATHER BRIEFS:

GARDEN VISITORS *(birds, insects, critters)*:

COLOR IN THE GARDEN:

SPECIAL PLEASURES:

LESSONS LEARNED:

TRIUMPHS:

DON'T FORGET:

PLAN AHEAD:

NOTES:

DATE:

TEMPERATURE A.M.:

TEMPERATURE P.M.:

WEATHER BRIEFS:

GARDEN VISITORS *(birds, insects, critters)*:

COLOR IN THE GARDEN:

SPECIAL PLEASURES:

LESSONS LEARNED:

TRIUMPHS:

DON'T FORGET:

PLAN AHEAD:

NOTES:

FALL

DATE: _____

TEMPERATURE A.M.: _____

TEMPERATURE P.M.: _____

WEATHER BRIEFS: _____

GARDEN VISITORS *(birds, insects, critters)*: _____

_____

_____

_____

COLOR IN THE GARDEN: _____

_____

_____

_____

_____

SPECIAL PLEASURES: _____

_____

LESSONS LEARNED: _____

_____

TRIUMPHS: _____

_____

DON'T FORGET: _____

_____

PLAN AHEAD: _____

_____

NOTES: _____

_____

_____

_____

_____

FALL

DATE:

TEMPERATURE A.M.: _____

TEMPERATURE P.M.: _____

WEATHER BRIEFS: _____

GARDEN VISITORS *(birds, insects, critters)*: _____

_____

_____

_____

COLOR IN THE GARDEN: _____

_____

_____

_____

SPECIAL PLEASURES: _____

LESSONS LEARNED: _____

TRIUMPHS: _____

DON'T FORGET: _____

PLAN AHEAD: _____

NOTES: _____

_____

_____

_____

_____

FALL

DATE: _____

TEMPERATURE A.M.: _____   TEMPERATURE P.M.: _____

WEATHER BRIEFS: _____   GARDEN VISITORS *(birds, insects, critters)*:

_____   _____

_____   _____

COLOR IN THE GARDEN: _____   _____

_____   _____

_____   _____

SPECIAL PLEASURES: _____

_____

LESSONS LEARNED: _____

_____

TRIUMPHS: _____

_____

DON'T FORGET: _____

_____

PLAN AHEAD: _____

_____

NOTES: _____

_____

_____

_____

_____

_____

_____

PURCHASE TOOLS

Toward Christmas, many stores selling gardening tools hold sales to make room for seasonal items. You want tools that will last, so when shopping for bargains, look closely at the tools and try them out. Large loppers can feel awkward and overbalanced, and certain shovels may be so heavy you will never want to use them. The strongest handles of tools are made from ash, and forged steel blades will stand up to the toughest job. Always try to buy the best-quality tool you can afford and plan to use it in your garden for many years.

MAKE MULCH LASAGNA

The colorful term "mulch lasagna" describes a system that allows you to fertilize and mulch at the same time, creating a barrier to weeds that may take as long as a year to break down. In late fall, when grasses are dying back and you are preparing the garden for winter, spread a thin layer of organic fertilizer and then cover the layer with newspaper. Totally cover the newspaper with either wheat straw or rice straw; the latter takes longer to break down. Straw, unlike hay, has few or no seeds, so it makes a better, weed-free mulch.

DATE:

TEMPERATURE A.M.:

TEMPERATURE P.M.:

WEATHER BRIEFS:

GARDEN VISITORS *(birds, insects, critters)*:

COLOR IN THE GARDEN:

SPECIAL PLEASURES:

LESSONS LEARNED:

TRIUMPHS:

DON'T FORGET:

PLAN AHEAD:

NOTES:

FALL

DATE:

TEMPERATURE A.M.: _____   TEMPERATURE P.M.: _____

WEATHER BRIEFS: _____   GARDEN VISITORS *(birds, insects, critters)*: ___

_____

_____

COLOR IN THE GARDEN: _____

_____

_____

SPECIAL PLEASURES: _____

LESSONS LEARNED: _____

TRIUMPHS: _____

DON'T FORGET: _____

PLAN AHEAD: _____

NOTES: _____

_____

_____

_____

_____

DATE:

TEMPERATURE A.M.:

TEMPERATURE P.M.:

WEATHER BRIEFS:

GARDEN VISITORS *(birds, insects, critters)*:

COLOR IN THE GARDEN:

SPECIAL PLEASURES:

LESSONS LEARNED:

TRIUMPHS:

DON'T FORGET:

PLAN AHEAD:

NOTES:

FALL

DATE:

TEMPERATURE A.M.:

TEMPERATURE P.M.:

WEATHER BRIEFS:

GARDEN VISITORS *(birds, insects, critters)*:

COLOR IN THE GARDEN:

SPECIAL PLEASURES:

LESSONS LEARNED:

TRIUMPHS:

DON'T FORGET:

PLAN AHEAD:

NOTES:

Gardener's Fall
CHECKLIST

○ Take advantage of fall garden sales to purchase shrubs and perennials.

○ Blanket tender plants with straw mulch to protect them from the coming winter cold.

○ Finish planting trees and shrubs at least six weeks before the date of the first frost. Water new plantings regularly in periods between rains.

○ Plant spring bulbs in garden beds or containers.

○ Turn out summer vegetable beds, add fertilizer and compost, and plant with garlic, leeks, and onions.

○ Set out winter flowers such as pansies, stock, and snapdragons.

○ Clean out vegetable beds from last harvest and plant with cover crops if you won't plant them with fall crops.

○ Trim back flowering and evergreen hedges to maintain their compact form.

○ Divide iris clumps if spring bloom seemed spotty.

○ Protect tuberous begonias and other tender bulbs from frost by digging them up and storing them in a frost-free area.

○ Wrap all exposed irrigation pipes with insulation to protect against early freezes.

○ Cut any asparagus fronds down to the ground.

○ Put away lawn furniture.

○ Clear leaf debris out of gutters and downspouts.

WARM REGIONS

- ○ Take advantage of fall garden sales to purchase shrubs and perennials.

- ○ Finish planting trees and shrubs at least six weeks before the date of the first frost. Water new plantings regularly in periods between rains.

- ○ Protect tuberous begonias and other tender bulbs from frost by digging them up and storing them in a frost-free area.

- ○ Blanket tender plants with straw mulch to protect them from the coming winter cold.

- ○ Cut any asparagus fronds down to the ground.

- ○ Set out cool-season vegetables for winter harvest.

- ○ Plant spring-blooming bulbs and cool-season annual flowers such as pansies, iceland poppies, and stock.

- ○ Put away lawn furniture.

- ○ Clear leaf debris out of gutters and downspouts.

HOT REGIONS

○ Begin garden clean-up: remove all spent plants, deadhead perennial borders, weed, and mulch.

○ If your microclimate risks cold snaps, dig up and store any bulbs that may be too tender to survive the cold.

○ Water less to acclimate plants to cooler weather.

○ Cut any asparagus fronds down to the ground.

○ Plant spring-blooming bulbs.

○ Plant deciduous trees and shrubs after leaf fall.

○ Plant out bare-root roses when available.

○ Plant out cool-season annuals and winter vegetables.

○ Clear leaf debris out of gutters and downspouts.

COLD REGIONS

- ○ Take advantage of fall garden sales to purchase shrubs and perennials.

- ○ If you plan to add deciduous trees or shrubs to your garden, visit nurseries, public gardens, or parks to check out their foliage colors and mature size.

- ○ Protect tuberous begonias and other tender bulbs from frost by digging them up and storing them in a frost-free area.

- ○ Cut perennial stalks down to 4 inches and spread winter mulches to protect perennial beds.

- ○ Prepare roses for winter: harvest rose hips, deadhead spent blooms, and mulch heavily for winter protection.

- ○ Plant spring-blooming bulbs.

- ○ Rake leaves into compost piles to decompose for spring mulch.

- ○ Clear leaf debris out of gutters and downspouts.

- ○ Buy bulbs of tazetta narcissus and set in water to force for indoor bloom.

- ○ Put away lawn furniture.

- ○ Drain gasoline from lawnmowers and store them under cover.

- ○ Drain irrigation pipes and wrap exposed hose bibs with insulation to protect against early freezes.

- ○ Prune all berry bushes.

GARDEN SKETCHES

GARDEN SKETCHES

GARDEN SKETCHES

WINTER

*Winter brings the gardener well-deserved
rest and time for reflection, while
outside the winds buffet the garden,
and the trees sway and dance.*

USE the quiet of winter to piece out what designers call the "bones" of next year's garden—the bare structure of edges, paths, and hard scape (such as patios or terraces), primary trees, and shrubs. Use your Garden Sketch pages (at the end of this chapter) to sketch out your main features. Label specific areas of your sketch, such as a main perennial bed or a rose circle, and note all of your garden's important flowers, bulbs, shrubs, and trees. Ask yourself whether you have enough places to rest, or whether adding a new bench might gain you a new view. Once you are sure of your goals, begin a wish list to consult once the garden catalogs begin to overflow in your mailbox.

Use this downtime to maintain your tools, whether they're a mish-mash jumble in a trug (a small carryall for the garden) or a heap of shovels and rakes in a corner of the garage. Make a shopping list of important items: gloves, garden twine (at least two balls), blade sharpeners, and splinter tweezers. Apply linseed oil with steel wool to the wooden handles of all your shovels, hoes, and pruners. Clean the blades of shovels and pruning saws, and thoroughly oil them to prevent rust. Sharpen pruning tools and the working edges of shovels, hoes, and weeding tools. Come spring, you will reap the reward of these endeavors when your blades cut crisply and your shovels dig easily.

Of course, there is no real downtime for gardeners. After storms, the garden must be surveyed for damaged branches and even downed trees. Check on stored plants every two weeks or so to be sure that they are hibernating without any problems. In warmer areas, gardeners should begin to prune in January, and, of course, you should choose bare-root plants and set them in the ground when weather and soil conditions allow.

Don't forget to take pictures of your garden on winter solstice day.

WINTER

DATE: _____

TEMPERATURE A.M.: _____

TEMPERATURE P.M.: _____

WEATHER BRIEFS: _____

GARDEN VISITORS *(birds, insects, critters)*: _____

_____

_____

COLOR IN THE GARDEN: _____

_____

_____

_____

_____

SPECIAL PLEASURES: _____

_____

LESSONS LEARNED: _____

_____

TRIUMPHS: _____

_____

DON'T FORGET: _____

_____

PLAN AHEAD: _____

_____

NOTES: _____

_____

_____

_____

_____

_____

WINTER

DATE:

TEMPERATURE A.M.:

TEMPERATURE P.M.:

WEATHER BRIEFS:

GARDEN VISITORS *(birds, insects, critters)*:

COLOR IN THE GARDEN:

SPECIAL PLEASURES:

LESSONS LEARNED:

TRIUMPHS:

DON'T FORGET:

PLAN AHEAD:

NOTES:

WINTER
DATE:

TEMPERATURE A.M.:   TEMPERATURE P.M.:

WEATHER BRIEFS: GARDEN VISITORS *(birds, insects, critters)*:

COLOR IN THE GARDEN:

SPECIAL PLEASURES:

LESSONS LEARNED:

TRIUMPHS:

DON'T FORGET:

PLAN AHEAD:

NOTES:

WINTER

DATE: _____

TEMPERATURE A.M.: _____

WEATHER BRIEFS: _____

_____

_____

COLOR IN THE GARDEN: _____

_____

_____

SPECIAL PLEASURES: _____

_____

LESSONS LEARNED: _____

_____

TRIUMPHS: _____

_____

DON'T FORGET: _____

_____

PLAN AHEAD: _____

_____

NOTES: _____

_____

_____

_____

_____

_____

TEMPERATURE P.M.: _____

GARDEN VISITORS *(birds, insects, critters)*: _____

_____

_____

_____

_____

_____

_____

WINTER

DATE: _____

TEMPERATURE A.M.: _____

TEMPERATURE P.M.: _____

WEATHER BRIEFS: _____

GARDEN VISITORS *(birds, insects, critters)*: _____

COLOR IN THE GARDEN: _____

SPECIAL PLEASURES: _____

LESSONS LEARNED: _____

TRIUMPHS: _____

DON'T FORGET: _____

PLAN AHEAD: _____

NOTES: _____

PLAN WITH RESTRAINT

Come December or January, the catalogs will start to pile up, with their irresistible pictures of lush flowers and appetizing vegetables. No gardener can resist buying, but be cautious when ordering your seeds or plants. Note their growing seasons and the number of days between transplanting and fruit or bloom.

Gardeners living in cool-climate growing areas must select early-season tomatoes or vegetables to get any produce during the summer. If you have a short growing season, cherry tomatoes and early-season vegetable varieties will reward you. Check the dates on lettuce, winter squash, corn, and eggplant. If you live with long, hot summers, plant early-, mid-, and late-season varieties to ensure a succession of harvests.

WINTER

DATE:

TEMPERATURE A.M.:

TEMPERATURE P.M.:

WEATHER BRIEFS:

GARDEN VISITORS *(birds, insects, critters)*:

COLOR IN THE GARDEN:

SPECIAL PLEASURES:

LESSONS LEARNED:

TRIUMPHS:

DON'T FORGET:

PLAN AHEAD:

NOTES:

DATE:

TEMPERATURE A.M.:

TEMPERATURE P.M.:

WEATHER BRIEFS:

GARDEN VISITORS *(birds, insects, critters)*:

COLOR IN THE GARDEN:

SPECIAL PLEASURES:

LESSONS LEARNED:

TRIUMPHS:

DON'T FORGET:

PLAN AHEAD:

NOTES:

DATE:

TEMPERATURE A.M.:

TEMPERATURE P.M.:

WEATHER BRIEFS:

GARDEN VISITORS *(birds, insects, critters)*:

COLOR IN THE GARDEN:

SPECIAL PLEASURES:

LESSONS LEARNED:

TRIUMPHS:

DON'T FORGET:

PLAN AHEAD:

NOTES:

DATE:

TEMPERATURE A.M.:

TEMPERATURE P.M.:

WEATHER BRIEFS:

GARDEN VISITORS *(birds, insects, critters)*:

COLOR IN THE GARDEN:

SPECIAL PLEASURES:

LESSONS LEARNED:

TRIUMPHS:

DON'T FORGET:

PLAN AHEAD:

NOTES:

WINTER

DATE: _____

TEMPERATURE A.M.: _____

WEATHER BRIEFS: _____

_____

_____

COLOR IN THE GARDEN: _____

_____

_____

SPECIAL PLEASURES: _____

_____

LESSONS LEARNED: _____

_____

TRIUMPHS: _____

_____

DON'T FORGET: _____

_____

PLAN AHEAD: _____

_____

NOTES: _____

_____

_____

_____

_____

_____

_____

TEMPERATURE P.M.: _____

GARDEN VISITORS *(birds, insects, critters)*: _____

_____

_____

_____

_____

_____

_____

DATE:

TEMPERATURE A.M.:   TEMPERATURE P.M.:

WEATHER BRIEFS: GARDEN VISITORS *(birds, insects, critters)*:

COLOR IN THE GARDEN:

SPECIAL PLEASURES:

LESSONS LEARNED:

TRIUMPHS:

DON'T FORGET:

PLAN AHEAD:

NOTES:

WINTER

DATE: _____

TEMPERATURE A.M.: _____

TEMPERATURE P.M.: _____

WEATHER BRIEFS: _____

GARDEN VISITORS *(birds, insects, critters)*: _____

_____

_____

_____

_____

COLOR IN THE GARDEN: _____

_____

_____

_____

_____

SPECIAL PLEASURES: _____

_____

LESSONS LEARNED: _____

_____

TRIUMPHS: _____

_____

DON'T FORGET: _____

_____

PLAN AHEAD: _____

_____

NOTES: _____

_____

_____

_____

_____

_____

MAINTAIN AND CONTAIN

For gardeners with terraces, window boxes, or balconies, containers offer a whole world of gardening. However, the small world of the container means you must pay extra attention to make sure that its resident plants' needs are met. Plants should be repotted every year, and you should refresh the containers with new soil mix and fertilizer. Water containers carefully, and, once a month during the growing season, add a liquid fertilizer, diluting it according to the directions, while the potting soil is moist from watering.

CULTIVATE PATIENCE

Enthusiastic after the inactivity of winter, gardeners itch to begin working in the garden. However, digging when the soil is too moist displaces its oxygen, compacts it, and disturbs its natural composition. To test your soil's readiness, dig a shovelful of soil, and if it falls off the back of the shovel in a wet clump, it is still too wet. Wait until the soil is moist but crumbly to start digging new beds or setting in bare-root plants.

WINTER

DATE:

TEMPERATURE A.M.:   TEMPERATURE P.M.:

WEATHER BRIEFS: GARDEN VISITORS *(birds, insects, critters)*:

COLOR IN THE GARDEN:

SPECIAL PLEASURES:

LESSONS LEARNED:

TRIUMPHS:

DON'T FORGET:

PLAN AHEAD:

NOTES:

WINTER

DATE:

TEMPERATURE A.M.: _____

TEMPERATURE P.M.: _____

WEATHER BRIEFS: _____

GARDEN VISITORS *(birds, insects, critters)*: _____

_____

_____

_____

_____

COLOR IN THE GARDEN: _____

_____

_____

_____

_____

SPECIAL PLEASURES: _____

_____

LESSONS LEARNED: _____

_____

TRIUMPHS: _____

_____

DON'T FORGET: _____

_____

PLAN AHEAD: _____

_____

NOTES: _____

_____

_____

_____

_____

_____

WINTER

DATE:

TEMPERATURE A.M.:   TEMPERATURE P.M.:

WEATHER BRIEFS: GARDEN VISITORS *(birds, insects, critters)*:

COLOR IN THE GARDEN:

SPECIAL PLEASURES:

LESSONS LEARNED:

TRIUMPHS:

DON'T FORGET:

PLAN AHEAD:

NOTES:

DATE:

TEMPERATURE A.M.:

TEMPERATURE P.M.:

WEATHER BRIEFS:

GARDEN VISITORS *(birds, insects, critters)*:

COLOR IN THE GARDEN:

SPECIAL PLEASURES:

LESSONS LEARNED:

TRIUMPHS:

DON'T FORGET:

PLAN AHEAD:

NOTES:

WINTER

TEMPERATURE A.M.:

TEMPERATURE P.M.:

WEATHER BRIEFS:

GARDEN VISITORS *(birds, insects, critters)*:

COLOR IN THE GARDEN:

SPECIAL PLEASURES:

LESSONS LEARNED:

TRIUMPHS:

DON'T FORGET:

PLAN AHEAD:

NOTES:

DATE:

TEMPERATURE A.M.:

TEMPERATURE P.M.:

WEATHER BRIEFS:

GARDEN VISITORS *(birds, insects, critters)*:

COLOR IN THE GARDEN:

SPECIAL PLEASURES:

LESSONS LEARNED:

TRIUMPHS:

DON'T FORGET:

PLAN AHEAD:

NOTES:

TRY ORGANIC GARDENING

If you haven't committed to organic gardening in your vegetable or ornamental garden, take time in the winter to read up on its advantages. Encouraging birds and beneficial insects to visit your garden and using only organic preparations, whether a homemade hot pepper solution or commercial soap spray, can control insect infestations. Healthy soil and good nutrition will strengthen plants' immunity to a variety of viral and fungal diseases. Choose plants that thrive in your specific soil and microclimate. When you decide to go organic, be sure to dispose of your shelf of pesticides and herbicides at local hazardous waste disposal sites.

WINTER

DATE:

TEMPERATURE A.M.: _____

WEATHER BRIEFS: _____

_____

COLOR IN THE GARDEN: _____

_____

_____

SPECIAL PLEASURES: _____

_____

LESSONS LEARNED: _____

_____

TRIUMPHS: _____

_____

DON'T FORGET: _____

_____

PLAN AHEAD: _____

_____

NOTES: _____

_____

_____

_____

_____

_____

TEMPERATURE P.M.: _____

GARDEN VISITORS *(birds, insects, critters)*:

_____

_____

_____

_____

_____

_____

DATE:

TEMPERATURE A.M.:

TEMPERATURE P.M.:

WEATHER BRIEFS:

GARDEN VISITORS *(birds, insects, critters)*:

COLOR IN THE GARDEN:

SPECIAL PLEASURES:

LESSONS LEARNED:

TRIUMPHS:

DON'T FORGET:

PLAN AHEAD:

NOTES:

DATE:

TEMPERATURE A.M.:

TEMPERATURE P.M.:

WEATHER BRIEFS:

GARDEN VISITORS *(birds, insects, critters)*:

COLOR IN THE GARDEN:

SPECIAL PLEASURES:

LESSONS LEARNED:

TRIUMPHS:

DON'T FORGET:

PLAN AHEAD:

NOTES:

TEMPERATURE A.M.:

TEMPERATURE P.M.:

WEATHER BRIEFS:

GARDEN VISITORS *(birds, insects, critters)*:

COLOR IN THE GARDEN:

SPECIAL PLEASURES:

LESSONS LEARNED:

TRIUMPHS:

DON'T FORGET:

PLAN AHEAD:

NOTES:

DATE:

TEMPERATURE A.M.:

TEMPERATURE P.M.:

WEATHER BRIEFS:

GARDEN VISITORS *(birds, insects, critters)*:

COLOR IN THE GARDEN:

SPECIAL PLEASURES:

LESSONS LEARNED:

TRIUMPHS:

DON'T FORGET:

PLAN AHEAD:

NOTES:

WINTER

DATE: _____

TEMPERATURE A.M.: _____

TEMPERATURE P.M.: _____

WEATHER BRIEFS: _____

GARDEN VISITORS *(birds, insects, critters)*:

_____

_____

COLOR IN THE GARDEN: _____

_____

_____

SPECIAL PLEASURES: _____

_____

LESSONS LEARNED: _____

_____

TRIUMPHS: _____

_____

DON'T FORGET: _____

_____

PLAN AHEAD: _____

_____

NOTES: _____

_____

_____

_____

_____

_____

WINTER

DATE: _____

TEMPERATURE A.M.: _____

TEMPERATURE P.M.: _____

WEATHER BRIEFS: _____

GARDEN VISITORS *(birds, insects, critters)*: _____

COLOR IN THE GARDEN: _____

SPECIAL PLEASURES: _____

LESSONS LEARNED: _____

TRIUMPHS: _____

DON'T FORGET: _____

PLAN AHEAD: _____

NOTES: _____

CONTROL SLUGS AND SNAILS

As the late-winter days warm into early spring, slugs and snails appear. Start early to eradicate these pests and protect your best daffodils and early-blooming plants from their hungry onslaught. In the early evening, armed with a flashlight and a sack with salt in the bottom, you can pick up the marauders as they begin to slime over your garden. This control method is not for the fainthearted. Alternatively, you can set out beer traps: a shallow can dug down into the soil so the top is even with soil level and then filled with beer. There are also effective organic commercial controls containing iron phosphate, a relatively nontoxic bait, that will not spread harmful pesticides in your garden.

TEMPERATURE A.M.:

TEMPERATURE P.M.:

WEATHER BRIEFS:

GARDEN VISITORS *(birds, insects, critters)*:

COLOR IN THE GARDEN:

SPECIAL PLEASURES:

LESSONS LEARNED:

TRIUMPHS:

DON'T FORGET:

PLAN AHEAD:

NOTES:

WINTER

DATE:

TEMPERATURE A.M.: _____

TEMPERATURE P.M.: _____

WEATHER BRIEFS: _____

GARDEN VISITORS *(birds, insects, critters)*: _____

_____

_____

_____

_____

COLOR IN THE GARDEN: _____

_____

_____

_____

_____

SPECIAL PLEASURES: _____

_____

LESSONS LEARNED: _____

_____

TRIUMPHS: _____

_____

DON'T FORGET: _____

_____

PLAN AHEAD: _____

_____

NOTES: _____

_____

_____

_____

_____

WINTER

DATE:

TEMPERATURE A.M.: _____

TEMPERATURE P.M.: _____

WEATHER BRIEFS: _____

GARDEN VISITORS *(birds, insects, critters)*: _____

COLOR IN THE GARDEN: _____

SPECIAL PLEASURES: _____

LESSONS LEARNED: _____

TRIUMPHS: _____

DON.'T FORGET: _____

PLAN AHEAD: _____

NOTES: _____

WINTER

DATE:

TEMPERATURE A.M.:   TEMPERATURE P.M.:

WEATHER BRIEFS: GARDEN VISITORS *(birds, insects, critters)*:

COLOR IN THE GARDEN:

SPECIAL PLEASURES:

LESSONS LEARNED:

TRIUMPHS:

DON'T FORGET:

PLAN AHEAD:

NOTES:

WINTER

DATE:

TEMPERATURE A.M.:

TEMPERATURE P.M.:

WEATHER BRIEFS:

GARDEN VISITORS *(birds, insects, critters)*:

COLOR IN THE GARDEN:

SPECIAL PLEASURES:

LESSONS LEARNED:

TRIUMPHS:

DON'T FORGET:

PLAN AHEAD:

NOTES:

"The right tool for the task" has been a catchphrase for years, and although there are all-purpose shovels for general garden tasks, there are also specialty shovels that help you accomplish jobs more efficiently. First find a shovel that is about as tall as you are. Then look for shovels that serve different purposes. A digging shovel has a straight shank, which is easy to step on when you're digging deep holes. A trenching shovel has a 6-inch head perfect for creating narrow trenches to plant asparagus roots or to set in pipes. An excellent shovel used for digging out stubborn weed roots and planting small bulbs has a miniature blade about 6 inches long. Search out different shovels and learn their various uses. They will ease your work in the garden.

PRUNE WHILE IT'S COLD

The deep cold of winter puts deciduous plants into such a stupor that even cutting off their limbs doesn't disturb them. Start pruning before spring warms the soil and starts the juices rising in these plants. All pruning tools, from handheld pruners to shears, loppers, and saws, should be oiled and sharpened before you set to work. Roses (excepting certain climbing roses and shrub roses), fruit trees, and deciduous shrubs should be pruned in late winter. Evergreen shrubs should be pruned later in the season, just before the weather warms and spring growth starts. Be advised that lengthy pruning sessions can tire your muscles and even cause carpal tunnel syndrome in overused wrists, so pace yourself in this work.

TACKLE MAINTENANCE WORK

Now that deciduous vines are sleeping, perennial shrubs have been pared back to their essential forms, and tall trees have been carefully pruned, you have the opportunity to make repairs that are impossible when summer's rampant growth obscures the bones of your garden. Repair fences, arbors, and walls exposed by the winter season. If need be, lean back climbing roses—they are amazingly limber in winter—and paint or repair behind them.

TEMPERATURE A.M.:

TEMPERATURE P.M.:

WEATHER BRIEFS:

GARDEN VISITORS *(birds, insects, critters)*:

COLOR IN THE GARDEN:

SPECIAL PLEASURES:

LESSONS LEARNED:

TRIUMPHS:

DON'T FORGET:

PLAN AHEAD:

NOTES:

DATE:

TEMPERATURE A.M.:

TEMPERATURE P.M.:

WEATHER BRIEFS:

GARDEN VISITORS *(birds, insects, critters)*:

COLOR IN THE GARDEN:

SPECIAL PLEASURES:

LESSONS LEARNED:

TRIUMPHS:

DON'T FORGET:

PLAN AHEAD:

NOTES:

WINTER

DATE: _____

TEMPERATURE A.M.: _____

TEMPERATURE P.M.: _____

WEATHER BRIEFS: _____

GARDEN VISITORS *(birds, insects, critters)*: _____

_____

_____

COLOR IN THE GARDEN: _____

_____

_____

SPECIAL PLEASURES: _____

LESSONS LEARNED: _____

TRIUMPHS: _____

DON'T FORGET: _____

PLAN AHEAD: _____

NOTES: _____

_____

_____

_____

_____

_____

WINTER

DATE: _____

TEMPERATURE A.M.: _____   TEMPERATURE P.M.: _____

WEATHER BRIEFS: _____   GARDEN VISITORS *(birds, insects, critters)*: _____

_____   _____

_____   _____

COLOR IN THE GARDEN: _____   _____

_____   _____

_____   _____

SPECIAL PLEASURES: _____

_____

LESSONS LEARNED: _____

_____

TRIUMPHS: _____

_____

DON'T FORGET: _____

_____

PLAN AHEAD: _____

_____

NOTES: _____

_____

_____

_____

_____

_____

Gardener's Winter
CHECKLIST

○ Spread 3 to 4 inches of mulch on garden beds to avoid excessive spring weeds.

○ Plant bare-root fruit trees and shrubs when weather allows. Bring pruned fruit-tree branches indoors and set in water to force blooms.

○ Note new spears of early bulbs and protect the earliest blooms from slugs and snails.

○ On Valentine's Day, sow seeds indoors for tomatoes, peppers, eggplants, melons, squash, and other warm-weather vegetables.

○ Dig and plant potato beds on St. Patrick's Day.

○ Shop for summer-blooming bulbs and annual seeds in catalogs and at nurseries.

○ Make sure to clean up dropped blossoms under camellias, as the decomposing blooms can spread camellia petal blight. Fertilize with an acid plant food after bloom finishes.

○ String exterior electric Christmas tree lights around citrus and other tender shrubs to protect them when temperatures drop.

○ Continue to harvest garden greens such as kale, chard, and lettuce.

○ Plant out cold-season annuals such as pansies, snapdragons, calendulas, and stock.

○ Mulch permanent plantings such as shrubs and trees to protect them from dry conditions.

○ Plant cool-season vegetable crops such as beets, carrots, radishes, and lettuce directly in the ground. Start tomatoes, peppers, and other warm-season vegetables inside.

○ Order onion and leek starts to plant after February 1.

○ String exterior electric Christmas tree lights around citrus and other tender shrubs to protect them when temperatures drop.

○ Make sure to clean up dropped blossoms under camellias, as the decomposing blooms can spread camellia petal blight. Fertilize with an acid plant food after bloom finishes.

○ Continue to harvest the winter vegetable garden. Renew beds of spent vegetables with fertilizer, add compost, and replant with cool-season early-spring crops such as cabbage, broccoli, kale, and chard.

○ Renew last season's spent vegetable beds with fertilizer, add compost, and replant with cool-season crops such as cabbage, broccoli, kale, and chard.

○ Prune roses, cutting back by about one-third. Clear out all crossing branches and prune back a few old center canes to prevent disease.

○ Trim off spent annual blooms to prolong flowering. Deadhead early spring–blooming bulbs but do not cut off foliage until it has yellowed and withered.

○ Trim back perennials after flowering to give a compact shape.

○ Start annual flower seeds and seeds of tomatoes, peppers, and other warm-season vegetables inside during the first week of January.

○ Plant potatoes on St. Patrick's Day and set out warm-weather vegetable seedlings and fast-growing annuals such as zinnias, cosmos, and marigolds.

○ As the weather warms at the end of winter, sow cool-weather crops such as radishes, peas, spinach, and lettuce.

○ Start summer bulbs such as caladiums, cannas, and begonias inside to plant outside after the last frost.

COLD REGIONS

- ○ Check your shrubs after heavy snowstorms and shake foliage to prevent snow loads from breaking branches.

- ○ Use sand, not salt, on icy paths so that after snow melts, excess salinity in the soil won't damage plants.

- ○ Start cool-weather vegetable seeds such as broccoli and cabbage indoors on Valentine's Day.

- ○ Tidy up the toolroom and use linseed oil on all wooden parts of garden tools. Sharpen lopper and pruner blades and the shanks of shovels, hoes, and weeders.

- ○ Order onions and leek starts to plant four weeks after the last frost.

- ○ Purchase bare-root plants: fruit and shade trees, strawberries, artichokes, roses, and deciduous shrubs.

- ○ Order spring and summer annual flower and vegetable seeds from catalogs or Web sites.

- ○ Order summer- and fall-blooming bulbs.

GARDEN SKETCHES

GARDEN SKETCHES

PLANTING PRIMER

SOILS, POTTING MIXES, AND PREPARED GROUND

Soil is a mixture of the three soil particles—clay, silt, and sand—plus any organic matter. Sand is chemically inactive, so it is the clay, silt, and organic matter that are involved in the complex exchanges of water and plant nutrients. Sand, however, is by far the largest of the particles, so its presence means that there will be correspondingly large spaces between soil particles. These very large soil pores contribute to good, fast drainage and high oxygen concentrations.

When you're growing plants in containers, a good-quality potting mix is critical: you need a soil medium that retains moisture, drains well, and won't become concrete-hard late in the summer. Commercial potting mixes have been sterilized, so they allow vegetable gardeners growing plants susceptible to soil-borne diseases, such as heirloom tomatoes, to avoid risk of infection.

A soil rich in organic matter, well composted and well rotted, contains a high level of microbial bacteria, the good bacteria that help keep soil and plants healthy and fight off bad bacteria that attack plant roots. For healthy plants, incorporate plenty of homemade or purchased compost into the soil before planting.

To plant in the ground, prepare the soil two to three weeks before your transplants will be ready to set out:

1. *If the soil is so wet that it falls off the shovel in clumps, wait for it to dry, or you'll risk compacting the ground, making it rock hard.*

2. *Once the soil conditions are right, remove unwanted weeds or plants.*

3. *With a shovel, a spade, or a machine such as a rototiller, add 4 inches of homemade or purchased compost, and organic fertilizer and turn the soil over to a depth of 12 to 18 inches. Water the turned soil, and allow any undesirable seeds that may be in the ground to sprout.*

4. *At a time when the ground is damp but not soggy, weed again, and use a hoe or shovel to break up any clods. Rake the surface smooth for planting.*

To plant in containers, purchase an all-purpose planting mix. Make sure to thoroughly soak the mix for at least an hour, if possible, before planting.

1. *Purchase containers with drainage holes in the bottom. Do not put rocks or gravel in the bottom of the container: contrary to common wisdom, this doesn't improve drainage. To keep out slugs and snails, place a small circle of screen over the drainage hole or holes.*

2. *Fill the container with potting soil halfway to the top. Set in the plant or plants. Add potting soil*

around the plant and fill the container to 1 inch from its top. Firm potting soil around the plant and water thoroughly.

3. *Adjust the height of the plant so that the top of its root ball is just at the level of the soil. If the plant is too low, tug gently on its leaves. If it sticks above the level of the soil, push it firmly down into the planting mix. Avoid handling plants by their stems, as you may injure them.*

4. *Feed with a liquid fertilizer diluted according to label instructions once a month during the growing season.*

5. *Water thoroughly but conservatively. Overwatering containers washes out nutrients and starves plants.*

WATER

Plants' circulatory systems use water to carry nutrients from the soil up through the stem to the leaves, flowers, and fruits. As water evaporates from the leaves, more water is drawn up by the roots, like a straw sucking up liquid. Plan to water your plants regularly, with the following exceptions:

1. *Plants need more water on excessively hot or windy days.*

2. *Sandy soils drain quickly, so plants in these soils may need more frequent watering.*

3. *Clay soils drain slowly, so plant roots may puddle and rot in underground water. Water such soils less.*

4. *Container plants have limited ground space and need more watering than plants growing in garden beds.*

FERTILIZERS

Like all living things, plants need food to grow. Plants absorb fertilizers in two ways, through their roots and through foliar feeding (spraying fertilizer on their leaves). Encouraging healthy roots is the first step in successful growing. If you see a stunted plant, pull it up, and you will find that its root development was thwarted either by insufficient water or nourishment or because the ground around the plant was inhospitable.

Fertilizer labels usually show three numbers, such as 20-6-12 or 5-5-5, which indicate their amounts of nitrogen, phosphorus, and potassium, respectively. These ingredients foster plant growth. Note: The higher the numbers in the formula, the stronger the fertilizer, and the less you need apply at any one time.

A dizzying number of commercial fertilizers are available. Chief among them are the following:

LIQUID FERTILIZERS: Synthetic or organic fertilizers, such as fish emulsion, need to be mixed with water and then applied. Too strong a solution can burn the roots of plants, especially new starts with fragile roots. You can apply weaker solutions more frequently, which may be ideal for container plants. You can also mix liquid fertilizers and spray them on leaves for foliar feeding.

CONTROLLED-RELEASE FERTILIZERS: These are synthetic or organic fertilizers that gradually melt over a specific length of time (noted on the label), feeding plants during the growing season. These are effective and easy to apply by mixing into the soil, but keep in mind that plants absorb fertilizer when the soil is warm, so apply them only after you've seen new growth in the spring.

SPECIAL FORMULA FERTILIZERS: Many plants have particular growing needs, and special formula fertilizers address these. Garden stores offer specially formulated fertilizers for acid-loving camellias and rhododendrons, low-nitrogen tomatoes, and high-nitrogen citrus, as well as other plants.

The cautious gardener, like the careful parent, keeps in mind that fertilizer is like candy: in the correct amount, it's a stimulating treat, but too much can injure the plant. Read the labels carefully and apply only as indicated.

STARTING FROM SEED

Don't hesitate to buy seed packets and start plants from scratch. Nurseries and catalogs sell hundreds more kinds of seeds than of plants. And seeds simply want to grow: many can be sown directly in the ground, and some can be scattered, covered with just a thin blanket of soil, and then watered. Learning how to start seeds also allows you to save your own seeds from open-pollinated plants (nonhybrid types whose seeds will replicate their parents'). Seeds from plants grown in your microclimate will adjust to your garden's soil and climate conditions, and after several growing seasons, they may become hardier than purchased plants trucked in from a regional growing center.

Many vegetable seeds are large and easy to plant. The rule of thumb is to plant the seed at a depth of twice its size. A zucchini seed is approximately a half-inch long, so it should be buried about an inch under the soil. Make sure to keep the soil of just-planted seeds damp to help the baby plants emerge.

If you live in a cold climate with a short growing season, starting seeds inside will produce vigorous plants ready for transplanting when the ground warms up. Sow seeds indoors about eight weeks before the date of the last spring frost in your microclimate. Other seeds can be sown directly in the ground later, after the summer's warmth has raised the ground temperature to a level that encourages germination. Seeds need an environment between 70°F and 85°F to germinate. To start seeds inside, plant the seeds about one-quarter inch deep in containers, water lightly, and cover with plastic to make sure the seeds do not dry out. An additional aid is a horticultural heat mat, which you place underneath propagating pots to provide bottom heat, which improves germination.

Sprouts of most plants will pop up in six to eight days. A sunny south window may provide enough light and warmth, or you can use Gro-Lights or full-spectrum lights positioned 4 to 6 inches above the containers. If your plants lean toward the light source and look skinny and weak, they are not getting enough light. After the plants develop their first true leaves, transplant them into 3- to 4-inch pots and place in an area with full light and temperatures of 60°F to 70°F. The plants should receive at least eight hours of sun a day, the more the better. Approximately seven to ten days before you want to transplant the plants outside, set them in a sheltered area outdoors during the day to accustom them to the outside environment. Bring them in or cover them at night to ensure late frosts don't nip the young and tender plants.

To transplant them outdoors into well-worked garden soil, use a spoon or a knife to dig out the plant and grasp it by its leaves, never its stem. Even the lightest pressure on the stem can damage a baby plant. Tuck the plant into its new home, firm the soil around the base of the plant, and water. If you are new to gardening, try growing summer squash, zinnias, or cosmos from seed to gain confidence in transplanting starts from seed.

Here's a starter list of easy-to-grow flowers perfect for starting from seed in midspring, after the threat of frost has passed:

ALYSSUM: very easy to grow, spreading groundcover with white flowers

CALENDULAS: Cheerful daisylike flowers in yellows and oranges

COSMOS: Many different types, but typically, a tall plant with shades of pink to white daisy flowers

NASTURTIUMS: Flowering vines that love the cool season, with edible flowers in oranges and pinks

SUNFLOWERS: Lots of choice between huge one-flowered plants and a range of colors including burgundy-flowered plants with multiple blooms

ZINNIAS: Tough cheerful plants with pinks and reds predominating, but try out the green flowered Envy.

VEGETABLE GARDENING

Busy lives might seem to preclude a sprawling vegetable garden, but, depending upon the size of your household, small plantings can supply you with delicious produce and homegrown satisfaction. Consider planting the following very easy-to-grow vegetables:

BEANS: Beans eaten raw just off the bush or vine can convince the most inveterate non-veggie eater to give vegetables a second chance. A summer crop, beans come in two forms, a bush type, which can even be grown in a container, or a vining type, which must be trellised. Sow successive crops over for a continual harvest. The purple- or yellow-podded beans are easiest to find among the foliage. Check dates to harvest to choose the best variety for your garden's growing season.

BEETS: Easily grown in the cool gardens of spring and fall, the versatile beet can be cooked for salads, pickles, soups, or as a side dish. Sow the beet seed thickly in rows or planted in beds and score two crops. Stir-fry the thinnings for their tasty green tops and wait to harvest the beet roots. You can harvest the beets when they are small or when they reach maturity. Beets are very successful for winter gardens in temperate winter areas, as they can stay in the ground without harm from frosts. Look for the steadfast heirloom

Red Bull, the red with white swirls Chioggia, or the delicate-tasting Golden beets.

CABBAGE FAMILY (CABBAGE, BROCCOLI, BRUSSELS SPROUTS): Those decrying the taste of cabbages have never raised their own. Home-grown cabbages are sweet when harvested out of the garden and cooked directly—unlike the supermarket types that might be months old. There are a host of different varieties with either compact heads or loose leaves, and a variety of Chinese cabbages. Broccoli, a member of the same family, produces a large main head. Cut that, and then wait for the smaller side shoots to continue the harvest, often over months. Brussels sprouts, a cool season crop with a long growing season seem to take forever before the sprouts begin to form, but resist harvesting the sprouts until they sweeten with frost. Begin to pluck off the sprouts when they are about 1-inch wide.

CAULIFLOWER: If you have extra room in your garden in early spring or late summer, try planting cauliflower. They are easy to start from seed and easy to grow, and the culinary rewards will startle the gardener used to purchasing weeks-old heads in the market. Look for varieties labeled self-blanching, so you don't have to tie the leaves around the head to keep it white. Spectacularly different are red cauliflowers or its delicious green cousin, Romanesco.

CARROTS: Carrots come in all colors of the rainbow, from the typical orange to yellow, white, and red. Their shapes can be round, short, and stubby or long and tapering. Every child, from five to seventy-five, loves carrots, and pulling them fresh from the garden is a real sweet treat. Start some in early spring and keep planting them through mid-summer. They like loose soil for their roots and constant moisture. You can grow carrots in containers if there is enough room for the roots to stretch down and you are sure to keep the soil moist.

COOKING GREENS (COLLARDS, KALE, SWISS CHARD, AND SPINACH): These hardy greens used to be thought pedestrian, until chefs began to exploit their deep, rich flavors pairing them with everything from duck to pasta. High in iron and folic acid, greens star in the kitchen in stir-fries and soups, and you can also grill them as an accompaniment to meat or braise them with olive oil and garlic to stuff into omelets. Greens are easy to grow, and many varieties will reseed themselves without any help from the gardener. Start plants in the early spring or again in late summer for a fall harvest. Collards love the summer heat but will also take chill temperatures. Cut only the outer leaves of a plant for continual production lasting for months. In mild temperature gardens, greens planted in the fall will produce until the heat of late spring causes them to bolt. Fordhook Giant and Rainbow chard are elegant choices for a garden bed, making a gorgeous show as annuals.

CORN: Corn takes room, and it must be planted in blocks for the best pollination. If you have the space, planting corn is easy, and the results delicious. Grilled fresh corn, still in the husk, is the very best dish of the summer garden. Corn cross-pollinates very easily, so for the best results, only plant one type of corn. Popcorn is a smaller corn, taking a smidgeon less space. You can follow the ways of Native Americans and plant the Three Sisters: interplanting corn, vining beans, and pumpkins. The beans climb up the corn, and the pumpkins fill all the spaces between the corn plants.

CUCUMBERS: You can train cucumbers on a trellis to save room in a small garden. Lemon cucumbers are round and tennis ball–shaped; Armenian cucumbers grow into long burpless cucumbers; while pickling gherkins should be picked at 2 or 3 inches long. Make sure to add plenty of fertilizer to the planting bed.

EDIBLE FLOWERS: These make your vegetable garden beautiful as well as productive—and who can resist the look of flowers in your food? Borage, a very easily grown herb with bright blue flowers, grows in the spring and will self-seed for more flowers in the fall. Johnny-Jump-Ups are easy to sow, and their tiny pansylike faces are charming in the garden as well as the salad. Nasturtiums sprout in the corners of container beds and provide gorgeous edible flowers to grace platters or add to herbed vinegars.

EGGPLANTS: There are so many new eggplants with colors ranging from white to deep purple and shapes from egglike to moon slivers. You will never get bored trying all the varieties. The smaller types will ripen in a cool summer garden; the larger need hot summer heat. They produce well in rich moist soil but will stand some neglect.

LETTUCE: No garden should be without salad greens. Quick and easy to grow in a row or a container, organically homegrown lettuce is handy for two or three leaves to include in a sandwich, or as a cut-and-come-again bed that will fill salad bowls for several months. There are many types that do well in summer heat, resisting bolting, and others that will stand up to chill spring and fall temperatures. Make sure to check the variety that will do the best in your climate and season. Mesclun mixtures combine several different types of lettuces in one package for an attractive variety of colors, textures, and tastes. They are often set to a particular season. Make sure to sow successive rows for a continual harvest. Remember, lettuce seedlings need to be protected from hungry birds and voracious slugs and snails.

MELONS: Melons sprawl, so garden space is essential, but, a space-worried gardener can train melons up a trellis, carefully, supporting the melons in slings when they form. Melons like heat, take a very rich soil, and want lots of water for the best success. Choose short-season melons for cool summer gardens or longer-growing melons if you have hot temperatures. Note growing seasons to choose varieties that will sweeten up in your climate.

PEPPERS: Peppers are heat-seekers, so cool summer climates have almost no hope of growing peppers. For those in warmer climates, peppers are upright plants, heavy producers, and you get to choose the culinary heat level, from sweet peppers perfect for salads to the blow-off-the-roof hot peppers, like serrano or habanero. Serving sweet, homegrown grilled peppers topped with a good olive oil and salt will win the chef-gardener instant approval among friends and neighbors. You can even grow pepper varieties (such as paprika, the fire-hot habanero, or the tamer poblana) to grind into powdered spices. In all cases, simply grind up fully ripened and dried peppers. The best peppers have a thick, fleshy wall, so that even when they're dried, there is plenty to grind into powder. Once ground, experiment with blends: add dried cilantro, dried coriander, or cumin seeds to your grinder.

POTATOES: Every gardener should try to grow potatoes. They succeed in almost any climate, but being a tropical plant, they must have some heat, and they will die back in frost. There are an astonishing variety of potatoes, from fingerlings, which look like a finger, to Yukon Gold with their golden flesh, to purple potatoes. Don't try to start sprouting potatoes from the supermarket, unless they are organic. Look for certified disease-free potatoes to plant in your garden so you won't introduce soil-borne diseases. Each potato has several "eyes" that will sprout. Cut large potatoes so there are at least two "eyes" per piece. Let the potatoes sit for several days to let the cut parts cure, or dry off. Smaller potatoes can be planted whole. Plant potatoes in a compost-rich bed. Harvest after plants flower and tops begin to die back.

RADISHES: It used to be that radishes were small red globes, but now they come in all sizes and colors. Radishes like cool weather and moist soil. The small round globes are easy to grow and quick to harvest—leave them too long and they get woody, but the roots will take longer. If you are short of room, grow radishes in containers. Pickled radishes, from the Japanese daikon to red-fleshed radishes make great accompaniments to sandwiches or salads.

SQUASH AND PUMPKINS: We must be judicious with squash and pumpkins, not over-planting and thus usurping garden space from a myriad of other vegetables or from trying different varieties each year. What choices the gardener faces, with summer squash, winter squash, and pumpkins, and all the plants need a generous amount of space. Summer squash varieties boggle the mind, with heirloom varieties as round as a bocce ball, or shaped like a trumpet, and winter squash in a rainbow of colors and shapes. Pumpkins, those darlings of Halloween, come in small, one-pie sizes, or large, that is gigantic, for pumpkin weigh-offs. Winter squash need a long season to produce and harden for long-keeping, but eating your own winter squash in January brings a gardener great pride. Make sure to note in the journal the varieties tested and their results and make sure to try different types every year.

TOMATOES: Gardeners with limited space should include at least a container of cherry tomatoes. A large container can hold two varieties of these candylike nuggets with all-summer production. Sun Gold is outstanding—small golden globes with intensely sweet flavor. If you have more room, try a variety of tomatoes in all colors and shapes. Evergreen and Green Stripey are delicious, and you will know they are ripe if they give to a gentle squeeze. Many heirloom tomatoes, such as Cherokee Black, Black Plum, or Black from Tula have skin tones of brown to burgundy and deep rich flavors. Hybrid tomatoes are bred to withstand certain soil-borne diseases, and may be easier for the beginner to start with. Check with your local nurseries for the best varieties for your climate. Don't start tomatoes too early, as they need warm soil to begin to grow.

THE HERB PANTRY

Growing herbs for the pantry needn't be an elaborate project like a knot garden or European parterre. You can easily grow three or four different herbs in one large container. Herbs are suited to container cultivation, and many with a Mediterranean heritage actually thrive on neglect. Every garden should include the following:

CHIVES: Members of the onion family, chives provide a subtle onion bite in a tablespoon scattered on top of cream soups or delicate fish dishes. Asian chives have long flat leaves and are often called for in stir-fries. Chives grow easily in the garden or in containers and have the second grace of edible flowers, delicious sprinkled in salads.

CORIANDER/CHINESE PARSLEY: The seeds of the annual herb coriander may be used in curries or as a pickling spice, but the stems and leaves, known as cilantro, are invaluable as additions to salsas and Asian dishes. Easily grown from seed, coriander grows well in cool seasons and tends to bolt in hot weather. There are some varieties touted as slower bolting, but come warm weather, and sooner or later coriander will send up flower stalks. Let the plant grow and harvest the seeds.

DILL: One of the easiest annual herbs to grow, dill fancies up potato salads, cold cucumber soup, pickles, and breads. The wispy foliage dries easily, and the immature seed heads are saved to add to the pickle jar. Leave some flowers to mature to seeds for use in herb breads.

FLAT LEAF ITALIAN PARSLEY: Stronger tasting than its curly cousin, flat-leaf parsley is easily grown in a deep container or a garden bed. Its leaves and stems are delicious additions to soups, stews, and pasta dishes, adding the benefit of taste and a wealth of vitamins and minerals.

GARLIC: Garlic heads are made up of many cloves, and each clove, when planted, will grow a whole head of new garlic. In mild winter areas, garlic can be planted in the fall to grow through winter and spring and then harvested in early summer. In gardens with hard frozen winter soil, plant garlic in the early spring. Plant each clove about 1 inch under well-enriched soil about 4 inches apart and keep moist throughout the growing season. As the temperatures warm up, and heads mature, withhold water. Harvest when the tips of the foliage begin to dry. Dig from the soil and let the heads cure in a shady spot for a week.

LEMON GRASS: A large, clumping tropical grass used in Asian cuisines and citrusy teas, this tender plant dies back when exposed to freezing temperatures. Plant it out in warmer climates but protect it as an indoor winter container plant in colder climates. Use gloves when harvesting, as the sharp leaves make tiny grass cuts.

OREGANO: Grown as a perennial in warmer areas, oregano is well known as the spaghetti herb, long loved by the Italians to flavor tomato sauces. Often confused with its cousin, marjoram, which has a sweeter flavor, oregano is one of the herbs in a bouquet garni mixture as well as many chili powders. Start with a plant, which will thrive in most any garden site, and harvest leaves all summer long.

ROSEMARY: Easy in a pot or as a medium-sized shrub, rosemary needs little attention in a hot, dry garden and is a great addition to any culinary pot. Althrough it is too tender for cold climates, plant it in a container that can be overwintered in a protected space. In warmer climates, grow the tall Tuscan Blue variety so you can use the branches as skewers for shish kebabs. In its creeping form, rosemary makes a useful groundcover or falls gracefully over ledges.

SWEET BASIL: Grow this annual in garden beds or containers so you can whip up pesto at a moment's notice. Look for Italian large leaf basil for pesto or try Thai basil for Asian dishes. Purple-leaved basil tints vinegar a delicious pink color and infusing bottles of basil vinegar is simple and a perfect gift for a cook. Simply harvest the mature basil, rinse to clean the leaves, and add to a bottle or jar of 5 percent white vinegar. Leave out on a countertop until the leaves stain the vinegar a delicate pink. Store in a cool dark place and use after two weeks.

SAGE: Glorious in the flower garden, some varieties have purple leaves, bicolored green-and-white leaves, or green-and-yellow leaves. Sage is vulnerable to frost, but it can be grown as an annual or overwintered in a warm spot. There are many different ornamental sages, known as salvias, available so make sure to buy culinary sage.

THYME: Gracefully drooping over a container's side or lining a garden pathway, thyme is easy to grow and comes in a variety of shapes, colors, and flavors. Any dish with a French accent calls for thyme. The small leaves make this herb particularly easy to dry. Just cut a handful, wash, and let the leaves and stems dry in the open air. Store in a jar in a cool dark place. When you are ready to use the dried herb, crumble the leaves into your recipe. Discard the stems.

RESOURCES

There are dozens and dozens of seed catalogs that sell plants, bulbs, and seeds. Here are just a few interesting suggestions.

BULBS

Brent and Becky's Bulbs
7900 Daffodil Lane
Gloucester, VA 23061
877-661-2852
www.brentandbeckysbulbs.com

White Flower Farm
P.O. Box 50, Route 63
Litchfield, CT 06759
800-503-9624
www.whiteflowerfarm.com

SEEDS

Bountiful Gardens
18001 Shafer Ranch Road
Willits, CA 95490-9626
707-459-6410
www.bountifulgardens.org

The Cook's Garden
P.O. Box C5030
Warminster, PA 18974
800-457-9703
www.cooksgarden.com

John Scheepers Kitchen Garden Seeds
23 Tulip Drive
P.O. Box 638
Bantam, CT 06750-0638
860-567-6086
www.kitchengardenseeds.com

Native Seeds/S.E.A.R.C.H
526 N. 4th Avenue
Tucson, AZ 85705-8450
520-622-5561
www.nativeseeds.org

The Natural Gardening Company
P.O. Box 750776
Petaluma, CA 94975-0776
707-766-9303
www.naturalgardening.com

Pinetree Garden Seeds
P.O. Box 300
New Gloucester, ME 04260
207-926-3400
www.superseeds.com

Seed Savers Exchange
3094 North Winn Road
Decorah, IA 52101
563-382-5990
www.seedsavers.org

Seeds of Change
1364 Rufina Circle, #5
Santa Fe, NM 87501
505-438-8080
www.seedsofchange.com

Southern Exposure Seed Exchange
P.O. Box 460
Mineral, VA 23117
540-894-9480
www.southernexposure.com

Territorial Seed Company
P.O. Box 158
Cottage Grove, OR 97424-0061
800-626-0866
www.territorialseed.com

Tomato Growers Supply Company
P.O. Box 60015
Fort Myers, FL 33906
888-478-7333
www.tomatogrowers.com

Totally Tomatoes
P.O. Box 126
Augusta, GA 30903-1526
706-663-9772
www.totallytomato.com

GENERAL REFERENCE SITES

American Horticultural Society (AHS)
www.ahs.org/master_gardeners
Among other things, the AHS has a map linking to information on every state's professional and amateur gardeners. Each state has a cooperative extension agency that distributes horticultural information to these gardeners.

Farmers' Almanac
www.farmersalmanac.com/
weather/a/average_frost_dates
Check to find your local frost dates, both first and last.

Fine Gardening
www.finegardening.com
This site offers a variety of helpful information plus useful plant lists.

Seed Swappers
www.seedswappers.com
Swap seeds, bulbs, plants, and information in this friendly forum.

INDEX